Out of the Darkness...

by

Mary Kloska

En Route Books and Media, LLC

St. Louis, MO

En Route Books and Media, LLC
5705 Rhodes Avenue
St. Louis, MO 63109

Cover credit: Mary Kloska

ISBN-13: 978-1-952464-52-2
LCCN: 2021930870

Scripture texts used in this work are taken
from The New American Bible,1987 by
World Bible Publishers, Inc.

Explanation of the Icon for the Cover

In this icon of Jesus' Passion, there are several things made visible to the heart. The first is His strong and passionate, yet gentle Love. The sensitivity of His Heart can be seen in His eyes as well as His body completely open in naked abandon. Jesus' Love is gentle, humble and yet strong. It is strong in faithfulness, yet gentle as it delicately respects people's freedom. His body is outlined in Blood, for His Blood is His greatest treasure and gift to mankind. Jesus' Blood calls and invites His children to come and drink at this His Heart's fountain of mercy, forgiveness, justice, and truth. Jesus' body is bruised—for He has been beaten to free His beloved children. And all is black around Him in this great night of the Cross—yet out from this darkness His Heart and Body Crucified in Love are a great Light to the world—a symbol of Love's conquering in the Resurrection. Jesus' Blood enlightens the way for hearts to find peace. It is the key to unlock all secrets hidden deep within—it is the balsam that will heal all wounded souls. More than words, Jesus' Love within this icon explains itself. This icon is the title to this book—it explains in beauty the truth of the words contained within. Yet the teachings inside of this work are much deeper than both these words and this icon—their truth can only be fully understood through Love. So, I pray that our Father grants His deep gift of Love in the Holy Spirit to each heart that will encounter this icon and this writing. And may His Love enkindle a fire of love within each soul, so that each may be made deeply one with Jesus by this wound shared from His Heart in the night. May Jesus bless you all in His Love. Amen.

Mary Elizabeth Kloska, Fiat +
Jesus' Little Wife, one with Him on the
　　Cross
Written on December 19, 2003

History of the Book

During Lent, 2003, I found myself alone at a mission station in Kansk, Siberia. I had been living in Krasnoyarsk, Russia, for 18 months, and the Bishop of our diocese decided that he wanted for the community I was working with to permanently take over the mission in Kansk, effective immediately. The religious sister with whom I was living decided to stay back (with a few short, random visits) in Krasnoyarsk to close up our apartment and finish some commitments we had at the parish there. It was agreed that I would move to Kansk and stay at the parish apartment alone. And yet, I was not alone— for during these months of solitude, I was granted permission to keep Jesus present in the chapel of the parish apartment. There was a priest nearby who would visit for Mass and then leave me with Jesus. But he was unable to have the Blessed Sacrament in his apartment because it was rented and would not be secure (considering the situation in Russia). This would mean that my apartment was the only place that the Blessed Sacrament was reserved for the 1000km stretch between Krasnoyarsk and Irkutsk. It was an incredible gift to have the Lord with me day and night, but it was also a responsibility to make my life one of total prayer. This wasn't as difficult for me to do as it would be for most people, for I had lived some time already with a hermit community in the US, and I had already felt called to a life of intense prayer. Spending 7-10 hours a day before the Lord was not new – for there had already been periods of my life when such long hours of prayer were necessary for me. And during this Blessed Lent, alone with Jesus in the Eucharist, the first part of this book you are reading now was opened up to my heart. I wrote this first part during those long hours in Kansk, with the hope that someday I could have it translated for the Russian people whom I so dearly love. I still have that hope.

After writing this book, I eventually shared it with a religious sister in Italy who translated it to use for the yearly Lenten retreat of her sisters. After that, it has 'rested in a drawer' while I strove to live it in the midst of my life as a missionary all over the world and as a hermit. It was only after many years lying dormant that the Lord encouraged me to try to get it published so that the riches I gained by writing it could also be shared with you.

The second part of this book was written during my 3-month stay living as a hermit in a ruin in the Tabernas desert of Southern Spain. It was written with the intention of guiding the reader deeper into union with Jesus' interior thoughts, feelings, and experiences during His Passion, Death, and Resurrection. I hope that as you take these words—using them as a retreat—and meditate on them in front of the Blessed Sacrament, you will come to know Our Lord's Love in a new way, and not only know it with your mind, but be touched in your heart and transformed into conformity with Him.

January 13, 2021

This book is consecrated to

Jesus' Sacred, Eucharistic Heart—
Pierced by our sins,
crushed by our offenses,
Offered as a perfect holocaust of Love
to gain for us Eternal happiness.
And to

His Most Holy Mother of Sorrows,
Who, with Her 'Twin Fiat' united to His
Own on Calvary, turned all bitterness to
sweetness by the embrace of Her Trustful
Surrender and Love.

Jesus, meek and humble of Heart and
Mary, Mother of Sorrows and Our Lady of
the Vine
—pray for us. +

This book is written for love of Jesus, my Husband. It is dedicated to and consecrated in His Blood, Obedience, Crucified Love, and Joyful Hope present in His Passion, Death, and Resurrection; and to His Sorrowful Mother, my Mother.

Here, at the beginning of this book, I do not want to explain myself too much (who I am or where I live or studied); instead, I would simply like to present this work as it is: as a collection of treasures Jesus has shared with my heart. In doing this, I hope to witness to the great power Jesus' Cross contains in itself.

My heart cringes at the thought of my interior life with Him being laid open so bare before the world, but I must remember that my Spouse was crucified naked—bearing all of Himself to the world and allowing us to reach out and touch His naked wounds so that we can know the fathomless abyss of His Love contained within them.

So, I must be 'naked' spiritually with Him, in order for you all to receive His Love in this intimate way. For Jesus gives such great gifts to be shared with all of His Church. I pray that who I am does not distract you from Who He is, for that is what He wants to show to you here. All I am is His little wife crucified one with Him on the Cross. He is everything in me. So, like St. Paul, I must simply live so that I can say, "I no longer live, but Jesus Crucified lives in me." I pray you meet Him here in these pages. Amen. Alleluia. Fiat.

These are not just words or theory, but something I have lived.

CONTENTS

PART ONE

I

Out of the Darkness…

"His judgment is sound who fears the LORD; out of obscurity he draws forth a clear plan." (Sirach 32:16)

The one who fears the Lord is weak as to himself. His strength is found in his weakness, for it is there that the power of God's great Love conquers. As one who is little and weak turns to His Father in Heaven in great trust, he is cared for by God faithfully in all his needs. The one who fears the Lord is full of wisdom. He has a listening heart, a heart that follows the Spirit's guiding voice and hand. And it is through this Spirit within him that he is able to find a clear path even in the midst of great darkness. Jesus is our Lord, but somehow mysteriously in His humanity He also trusted in the Lord. It is about Him that the Psalmist writes, "But I am afflicted and in pain; let your saving help, O God, protect me. I will praise the name of God in song, and I will glorify him with thanksgiving." (Psalm 69:30-31). It is in Jesus' great Love for and trust in His Father, ultimately shown in His surrender in the weakness of the Cross, that we see how God never abandons those children of His who trust and fear Him in love. It is in the darkness of the Cross that the Father's plan of Salvation is carried out. It is in Jesus' weak littleness on the Cross, offered to the Father in Love, that the Father carries out His great plan to conquer death and sin. It is out from the darkness, obscurity and pain of the Cross that we are healed, saved and guided by Jesus' clear Light of Love. It is from His Death that we are given Life. And so as we unite with Him in deep Christian Love, we will come to be one with Him in His dark Love. It will be from within the dark, unclear places of our lives that the Father's faithful Hand will guide. It will be from our little deaths in life that God places His Life within us. It will be from our weakness, offered to the Father, where He will place His powerful Crucified and Resurrected Love. This is our hope and our joy: that out, from the darkness in our lives, He will draw forth a rich plan of His Love. In this, we will be like His Son Jesus.

II

Darkness, Stillness, and Silence

*"From noon onward, darkness came over
the whole land until three in the afternoon."*
(Matthew 27:45)

The moment of the Crucifixion is a
moment that touches each of our lives deeply.
It is the moment of God's unfathomable Love
to us: the moment of our Salvation. It is a
moment of darkness, of stillness, and of
deafening silence – three things which our
modern world runs from, seeing them as evil.
The beauty of the Cross' darkness is in the
veiling of a mysterious Love—our Savior's
Love– both fully human and divine. His Love,
which carried Him through the Crucifixion,
is not understandable to the human mind,

but it is known by its presence deep within the human heart open in faith.

Why is God's wonderful Love in the Crucifixion surrounded by darkness and obscurity? Darkness cleans our hearts, making room for the sublime. Darkness opens us, allowing for us to be uncovered without shame. And it is in the interior darkness of the soul (a darkness that fills one's mind, emotions, memory and heart) that God is able to undress humanity from its many masks to unite with her in deep Love.

Why was God's greatest act of Love held bound in the stillness of the Cross? Stillness is also something the modern human mind considers evil in a world where work and motion are our gods. And yet it is only in stillness that we can receive the work of God's Love to our hearts. It is in stillness that we hear Him and are filled with Him in peace. Our hearts search for stillness in the midst of our moving world. In the morning, for example, as we wait for our coffee to brew (so we can have energy to work and move all day) our hearts may encounter a moment of naked stillness in which God can give peace. It is in little moments like these that Jesus is reaching out to us from the Cross to join us to Him in simple suffering Love. **Jesus could not do much on the Cross because His hands and feet were crucified– but it was in this great act of still surrender and Love that we were saved. What we do is not as important as how much we love.** Waiting for coffee to brew in love does more for the world than feeding the poor without charity. This is the truth that Jesus' stillness on the Cross reveals to us.

Silence is something almost non-existent in our world of computers, TV and radio. Silence leaves us still and naked with ourselves and so we avoid it like a plague. And if our modern-day humanity runs from physical silences, how much more do we lack in interior silence. Real silence is not of the mouth or ears, but of the mind and heart.

Real silence is full of love, or listening attentiveness to the Face, Heart, words and desires of the Beloved.

And God takes these three things so shunned in our modern-day world—darkness, stillness, silence—and within them reveals to us the greatest mysteries of His Love: Crucified. From the Cross He uses darkness, stillness and silence as instruments to give the greatest Light, to do the greatest Act and to speak a word that has rung in people's minds and hearts for all generations. "Out of obscurity He draws forth a clear plan...." (Sirach 32:16). That is how God has always worked. In the night of Abraham's old barren age, He built up a great nation, as countless as the stars. In the moment Isaac was to be sacrificed in obedience, He sent an angel to rescue him. In the lonely wilderness when Jacob slept on a rock, the Lord came and spoke to him, promising him many descendants. And only after the angel wrestled with him, injuring Jacob in the hip, did Jacob receive his blessing. Joseph was sold into slavery, yet from the pit of his jail cell God lifted him up to be a great helper to Pharaoh and a savior to his family. After years of slavery in Egypt, God rescued His people, saving Moses from the sword and calling him forth to guide the Israelites to the Promised Land. In the desert God split the Red Sea to save His people; He provided water from a rock and bread from the heavens. Three times in the night Samuel heard God calling to Him. And Jonah heard God speak to him in the belly of a whale. Daniel was thrown to the lions, yet not a bone of his body was harmed and all the people praised the One True God on account of His faithfulness in the night. From the dark night of faith which Joseph, the husband of Mary, suffered, God revealed His great plan to him in a dream. And twice he was warned through a dream in the night to go to Egypt and to return to Nazareth so that the Christ Child would be safe. It was precisely in the night, in stillness, in silence from which God spoke to His people and delivered them. Jesus, from the dark night of the Cross, gave Life to all people. That is how God worked in the mystery of Salvation. And that is how He works in each of our lives today.

Yes, God, as a Person, as a Father, as the Son, as the Beloved, as a Shepherd, as Wisdom, as a Spirit, is active – striving to have a deep relationship with each of us His children and His beloved, today. His thirst for our love is evident in our lives through our encounters with darkness, stillness and silence, as He strives to strip us from the masks of image, advertising and our own perceptions, in order to transform us into living images of Crucified Love with His Son. Why is His Crucifixion so beautiful? Because it is naked truth – it is the purest of selfless loves. The Crucifixion is so necessary to wake us up, to open us, to heal us, to strengthen us. Jesus' Crucifixion brings us to God and so it is the means through which we find peace, joy, hope. In His Blood is our peace. "For in him all the fullness was pleased to dwell, and through him to reconcile all things for him, **making peace by the blood of his cross...**" (Colossians 1:19-20). Yes, that is what His Crucifixion does – it is a Love so pure, it gives us great peace. And it gives us the possibility to find great peace in our little sharings of His Crucifixion with Him in our daily crosses.

The darkness of Calvary gives meaning to the Light of the Resurrection. It shows the strength of merciful Love. We cannot live only in the Resurrection, because our hearts are not deep enough, open enough yet to receive this gift. The Resurrection is even around us, but it cannot be lived deeply until we embrace the Savior's Kiss of Crucifixion, darkness, stillness and silence in our lives. It is here, in the depths of Jesus' dark, still Heart on the Cross, that we are purified and stripped in order to receive His Love. It is here He is able to give His strength to fill us. We must always see the Crucifixion and

Resurrection together in our lives. **Without the Resurrection there is no hope. But without the Crucifixion, there is no Love.** We must live the Crucifixion with Jesus in the little ways He offers us every day, and also live with Him in His Resurrected Love. In this we become images of Him, of His Heart, living in the world. In this we find union with Him. In this we are changed into His Love living on earth.

Love is a concrete thing lost in this world. It is death to self for the Beloved and His presence in others. It is service through attentiveness to Jesus' needs in others. It is allowing His Love to live in us – which means perfect forgiveness, perfect obedience, perfect poverty, perfect chastity, perfect fiat. In perfect I mean perfectly according to the way that the Father has willed for us to live His Love. Each person is called to let Him enter into himself to live like this. This sort of Love, Jesus' Love Crucified and Risen, is a Love beyond death. It is a Love that conquers death and carries us forward to live with Him in His Heavenly Kingdom.

III

This is My Body...

On the night before Jesus died, He gave to us the gift of Himself in the Eucharist. He said, *'This is My Body, which will be given for you; do this in memory of Me... This cup is the new covenant in My Blood, which will be shed for you.'* (Luke 22:19b, 20b) As these words show, there is a deep connection between the Eucharist and the Cross. The gift of Jesus' Body and Blood, Soul and Divinity in the Eucharist is the gift of His Crucified Heart. And this Heart is real. Jesus gives us in the Eucharist and on the Cross the gift of His Body. It is not only the gift of His Body and Soul crucified for our sins, for our salvation, as an offering for us to the Father, but also is the gift of Himself to us. Jesus surrendered

His Body on the Cross as a gift to us. His
union with us from the Cross and in the
Eucharist is two-fold. One, He takes upon
Himself our sufferings and in this we are
united. But also He simply offers Himself on
the Cross in a marital gesture of Love. And
this offering on the Cross we receive to
ourselves in the Eucharist. Here, Jesus open,
vulnerable, weak and naked says, *'Here is My
Body– receive Me and let us be one. Here is
My Blood, given as a gift for you, and to you.'*
In the Eucharist we receive the Marital Love
of Jesus, the gift of His body for us and to us.
And as the true Spouse of each of our hearts,
Jesus not only offers us His Body on the Cross
and in the Eucharist, but also His soul – all
He is. Jesus suffered intensely within Himself
–His interior sufferings more anguishing
than His exterior– for Love of us and to be a
gift to us. In the Garden Jesus said, *'My soul
is sorrowful even to death.'* (Matthew 26:38).
And from the Cross He cried, *'Eli, Eli, lema
sabachthani? which means, My God, My*

God, why have you forsaken me?' (Mt 27:46). These both reveal a tiny piece of the mysterious interior anguish Jesus suffered on the Cross. He offered His Heart, His soul, His emotions—all—as a sacrifice for our redemption. And it is in these interior sufferings that Jesus became one with our hearts and the mysteries of our hearts' deep sufferings and wounds. Here on the Cross and in the Eucharist Heart meets heart— Wound meets wound—His Gift meets our gift of self to Him and with Him for the world. For love is a dialog. There is always a question and an answer. The highest example of this is the Trinity, Who is Love. The Father loves the Son, the Son answers and loves the Father. The Love which questions and answers between them is the Holy Spirit. When two people love each other this is also seen. One person speaks, the other listens and then answers. One person does something kind and the other receives and offers another kind gesture back. Love lives, creates, speaks. And this is true of Jesus' Eucharistic Crucified Love as well. He offers His Body to us, and we must receive Him, and answer Him by offering our body to Him. This is how Love forms union. The Trinity is one in Love and Jesus calls us to share in this Love with Him. *'This is My Body,'* He says, and He empties Himself fully for us on the Cross and in us in the Eucharist. He gives us His wounds as a place to rest ours. He gives us His Heart as a place for ours to live. He suffers interiorly as an emptying of Himself for us and He calls us, as we answer His Love by receiving Him to ourselves, to be united with Him in Love and to offer ourselves with Him.

Jesus was naked on the Cross. This is a fact that many are afraid to admit, fearing that nakedness would make our Savior impure. But purity does not come in clothes – purity is the presence of God in the heart. Little babies are born pure and naked – untouched by all not of God. Jesus was so pure as a little, naked child on the Cross, for

He was full of the presence of God – He *was* God. Jesus was naked on the Cross not only in His Body, but also in His Heart. And this is how we meet Him in the Eucharist as well: naked – pure gift of Love. Jesus' nakedness is a sign of His vulnerability in Love, in His Love so great for us that He was willing to give all, reveal all. Clothes on His body or 'clothes' on His Heart would have separated us from Him. He reveals all of Himself to us from the Cross and He says, *'This is My Body, This is My Blood, This is My Heart and Soul – take it, receive Me into yourself. I want to be one with you.'* In this we see the most perfect act of Marital Love. As a husband and wife desire to give all of themselves to each other—exteriorly and interiorly—so Jesus desired to give Himself to us on the Cross in such perfect Marital Love that human marital love is only a shadow of this Reality. As a husband and wife are pure in their nakedness before each other—full of pure love and desire to selflessly give the fullness of themselves—so too Jesus was pure in His naked act of Crucified Marital Love. And so, as we receive Him in the Eucharist, He calls us to receive His gift, His humble weakness and littleness of His Body in the form of bread and wine, so that we may have the strength to give of ourselves in little, naked weakness to Him as well. Jesus knows that we need His Body. We need His Body for life, for salvation, for healing, for peace and for Love. He also knows that our pride or fear or defenses often prevent us from allowing His Body to touch ours, especially in our places of wounds. And so He becomes wounded for us, to call us, to open us, to heal us and be united with us.

It is difficult to not answer real Love. The human heart was made for God, to respond to His Love. And so, it is very difficult for a person to be inundated with Love and not be affected. Especially when that Love is so one with us in humanness and, yet, divine. Jesus from the Cross, especially as given to us in the

Eucharist, inundates us with Love, consuming us, so that we will respond in opening ourselves, our wounds, our sins to His healing Love. In this, in Him, we find the Spring of strength that we need to live united with Him in the Father.

Jesus' wounds and His Cross spoke of the Resurrection – for He hoped and believed in the terrifying darkness. His wounds give life because they were resurrected. And so, as we unite with Him on the Cross in our lives and in the gift of Himself in the Eucharist, we will be filled with the strength of new life, of faith, hope and His joyful resurrected Love as well.

IV

Shadows of the Cross...

There is no worse feeling, I think, than of
being afraid, especially when we feel afraid
and without any defenses. There is fear which
we can control – for example, by reasoning to
ourselves that there is no reason for fear. Or
there is fear that can be overcome by faith
through prayer. Yet there is other fear which
sometimes overtakes a person – maybe
without good reason. The will of a person
may desire to trust and have faith in God's
Love and protection, but somehow fear
seems to grip his emotions all the more. This
sort of fear is almost evil – a great temptation
of the devil to lose faith, hope and trust in
God. And this sort of fear that comes in deep
darkness griping one's mind is the fear that

Jesus suffered in His Heart on the Cross. Yes, Jesus fully surrendered to the cup that the Father gave to Him, yet fear still clung to His soul. In the Garden of Gethsemane, as He was praying for the grace to endure all before Him, Matthew's Gospel says that He prayed, *'My Soul is sorrowful even unto death. Please remain here and keep watch with me. He advanced a little and fell prostrate in prayer saying, 'If it is possible let this cup pass from me; yet not as I will, but as you will.'* (Matthew 26:38-39) St. Luke tells us that *'He was in such agony and He prayed so fervently that His sweat became like drops of blood falling on the ground.'* (Luke 22:44) To be gripped by such fear is a horrible thing, yet usually having someone with us in such times can help to disperse the deep feelings of terror. Yet as Jesus three times returned to His disciples during His agony He found them asleep while He was suffering intensely. Jesus felt deep loneliness in His suffering. And not only in the Garden, but also on the

Cross Jesus suffered all of His horrible fear alone. Yes, it is true that the Father sent an angel to comfort Him in the Garden, and that His Mother, some women and His beloved disciple stood by the Cross; and these all were deep comforts in themselves. Yet if Jesus truly took all the sins, suffering, fear, temptations, and aloneness of humanity upon Himself in the Cross, then in His body, emotions and mind He truly did feel abandoned. People who loved Him may have been present, but the darkness prevented Him from receiving this love around Him. He sacrificed it as He took our sin and suffering upon Himself. In this He was able to unite with those most abandoned on earth. Jesus believed in the love around Him, but this love could not be felt or seen by His faculties. The devil was able to tempt Him fully in His mind, emotions and body. Darkness was allowed to swallow Him. This depth of His suffering is a mystery of His Love.

Fear is also intensified by darkness. St. Luke writes, *'It was now about noon and darkness came over the whole land until three in the afternoon because of an eclipse of the sun.'* (Luke 23:44) Darkness not only covered Jesus physically, yet also mentally and emotionally as He was abandoned and tempted; a deep spiritual darkness entered Him as well, as His Father also seemed to have left Him. The Cross was the hour of the darkest night. Jesus was left alone to endure through the imperceptible Love of His Father, in which He faithfully believed and obeyed. St. John writes that *'Perfect love casts out all fear.'* (1 John 4:18) This is true of the heart. When the heart believes, when the heart is open in love to receive God's Love, such Love frees, untangles in a way, the depths of a soul from fear. Yet, the devil can still haunt a person's emotions or mind with the darkness and feelings of fear. He cannot touch their heart, where God's Love reigns, but He can bother those other faculties of a person if God so allows. This is the sort of experience that Jesus suffered in the Passion. He took all of our suffering on Himself, and that included the dark night of our fears. When He took our sins upon Himself, He allowed His eyes to be blinded from seeing the Father's Love and this is a torturous experience. When He took our wounds upon Himself, He took those wounds of our hearts that make them incapable of receiving the fullness of God's Love, which casts out all fear. (Even if at the same time He remained united to His Father by accepting His will in Fiat.) Oh the horror His Crucified Heart suffered in drinking the cup of our fears! How the devil tortured His lonely Heart in this!

And Jesus, in His great purity of Heart, suffered more from this darkness, sin and fear than we could ever conceive. Jesus, although He was a man, had a heart of a little child – for His Heart was so pure He was greatly sensitive to all emotions, situations and people. His Heart was able to acutely take everything in deep to its core, and this includes the evil He consumed for us on the Cross. His Heart was so pure; it was defenseless. He was open completely on the Cross in vulnerable Love so as to drink fully the Father's will and so to receive all of humanity deep into Himself. Yet this openness caused the terror of His Cross to be even greater, for He had no defenses against His fear. He had no visible security except for the nails securing Him to the Cross.

And there is nothing like a person being naked when he is afraid. When one fears, the temptation is for us to cover ourselves, to hide or defend ourselves. When a child is afraid, he often puts covers over his head. Jesus, haunted by fear on the Cross, hung there naked and pierced open before the whole world. He was defenseless, yet this was a sign of His deep Love. He did not hide Himself and He did not try to defend Himself. He laid Himself open, bare before the world even in His fear for the sake of Love. Yet He remained faithful, believing underneath the horror of the Crucifixion, deep in His Heart, that the Love of the Father would carry Him. This is Love. This is Crucified Love: The willingness to take all of hell upon oneself in order to free the beloved (who is you, me and all of humanity) into the Father's Eternal Love. Jesus never ran from suffering. But as we see in the Gospel He went out to greet it and received it to Himself as a precious gift to free the world. He said, *"Shall I not drink the cup that the Father gave me?"* And we see in the Garden that "Jesus, knowing everything that was going to happen to him, went out and said to them, '*Whom are you looking for?*' We are so unworthy of such great Love running forward to save us. And His Love, as we see in this, was great.

The abandonment Jesus suffered in all of this terror of the Cross greatly intensified His pain. To suffer alone is so difficult, and how much more difficult to suffer alone when one feels abandoned. Jesus cried from the Cross, *'My God, My God, why have you abandoned me?'* Yes, even His good Father in Heaven seemed to have abandoned Him in His darkest hour. He was in terror and excruciating pain seemingly alone. Yet He still believed and He still loved. He kept His eye on the Father's will for His life so that He knew the precise moment He had fulfilled all. He said in that moment, *'It is finished.'* And He gave up His Spirit to His Father.

Jesus' Mother stood faithful at the foot of His Cross, yet it must have been hard to see Her with the blood that filled Christ's eyes. He had to believe in Her love. Seeing Her in grief had to have added to the torture of His pain. Feeling helpless on the Cross to comfort Her –watching Her below– must have torn His Heart. St. John writes, *'When Jesus saw His mother and the disciple there whom he loved, he said to his mother, 'Woman, behold your son.' Then he said to the disciple, 'Behold your mother.''* (John 19:26) In these flashing moments that Jesus did see His Mother, He must have received great comfort in Her presence. And yet there, in the moment He saw the comfort of His Mother's glance and love, He did not keep Her love of Him for Himself. In that moment of comfort He gave up His comfort as a most precious gift to us. He gave Her to us. What wondrous Love is a Love Crucified.

The suffering that Jesus suffered both physically as well as internally on the Cross was of the most intense kind—for it was a suffering leading to death. When a body is hurt, or the heart is wounded, right away it naturally begins the fight to be healed. The pain that was so tangible at first seems to be lessoned after a few days or weeks, fading as our body and heart adjust to it and begin to defend ourselves. Usually we can find some goodness in a person or a grace to make it easier to bear after the first blow. Yet Jesus' suffering in the Passion was different. I don't know if He knew He would suffer on the

Cross for three hours, or if it all simply seemed endless while He endured, but either way He had no watch to count down the minutes. He simply had to drink every drop that came to Him. And His suffering seemed new in every minute. Each suffering was added to by new fresh sufferings every minute – both internally and externally. When we read about the physical suffering in the Cross, the body is every minute crushing under new pain of collapse, leading eventually to death. And Jesus' new, physical pain in every moment was added to by His pierced Heart and soul through His nakedness, abandonment, disappointment, betrayal, insults, other's misunderstanding, darkness, temptations and separation from His Father. His pain was acutely new, fresh in every moment and seemingly without end. Three hours is a long time to hang on the Cross, especially as Jesus stared out at a black world rejecting His Love. Yet He received all of it fully to Himself, without defense, out of

Love and obedience to the Father and out of Love for us.

As Jesus shares bits of such suffering with us, we should find comfort in the fact that we can be with Him – our lonely, abandoned, crucified Lord. In these moments that we suffer with Him, we quench His thirst for love. All we have to do is fiat, deep in our hearts, to His Heart-wound's kiss in the darkness, abandonment and fear that seems to grip our lives at times. We must find comfort, at these times, in Him. For He suffered all this alone so that we never had to suffer alone. His loneliness gives us strength and the comfort of His presence in our fear and pain.

Oh Jesus, teach us to love as You do. That is all we can pray. Help us to be faithful in love as You were. May our lives wipe Your tears of blood. May our little fiat with You be a tender kiss to Your Heart, crucified open in Love. We want to love You. We need to love You, especially in this moment of Crossed Love, when heaven above and the whole earth below seemed to have left You alone in Your great shadow of sorrow. Help our lives be an answer of love in response to Yours. Please send us the Holy Spirit to set us on fire with Your Love, trust and faithful hope from the Cross, so that in the midst of our sufferings, we may look with You on the Cross away from this world which withers away quickly and into the great joy of Eternal Life with You in the Resurrection. Amen.

V

Nails

What are the nails in Jesus' hands and feet? Metal pressed through human flesh. What about the nails piercing His Heart, nailing His Heart to the Cross as well? These nails are not visible, but equally (if not more) painful. Nails are powerful things, but only if used by humans properly they are only strong if humans exert the force of a strong blow against them. Nails are very concrete things, and so were the nails that pierced Jesus to the Cross. They were very concrete and gave Him concrete pain. The Cross, the Crucifixion, the Passion, are not just abstract ideas good in guiding one's mind in a pretty meditation. No, Jesus' pain was concrete – just as the nails in His hands and feet were concrete– just as the shadows of His Passion that fall upon our lives are concrete situations, people, words and sufferings. Jesus' pain in His Heart –the nails that pierced His Love– were very concrete as well, even if they were not visible. These nails that crucified His Love were concrete words and actions of sin committed against Him and against His Father. They were concrete rejection and abandonment. They were concrete darkness, confusion and temptation which consumed Him on the Cross. These nails were more painful than those nails that pierced His body physically – for the force which drove the nails into His body was a soldier and a hammer. The force that drove the nails into His Heart was the sin of the hearts of His Beloved people and the darkness of Hell itself unleashed on Him. Jesus shares His Cross with us. It is His precious gift of Love—for it deepens our hearts with a thirst for Him. In the Cross, we—weak, little humanity—cannot endure alone. And so in the Cross we find a deep encounter with Love—bending down in mercy and reaching out in forgiveness from the Cross to carry us, heal us, save us. The Cross was not fun. And our crosses are not fun. But they are the beds that birth forth Love—true, pure Love. They give our hearts a chance to be perfected in Love—a Love emptied of self, seeking good for all—even those who crucify us. Jesus offered this type of Love to the soldier, piercing His side with a sword, as well as to those piercing His Heart in sin. Jesus always offered goodness to those who did bad. He always offered kindness. He always offered mercy.

In our lives, Jesus meets us in the Cross. He did not come to die on the Cross to take away our suffering. No, He loved too much for that. Love seeks to be united to the beloved, and for the perfect Man-God to unite us to Him He had to allow for us to be free to love. His Father did not want His creation to be robots. No, He wanted them to have hearts to share in new life and love. And so He made us free. And people will misuse this freedom—almost all people have—to choose against love. And in this is sin. And in this we encounter the nails of Jesus' Cross piercing us as well. The nails of Jesus' Cross also pierce us through sickness. And why does this type of Cross enter our lives? Couldn't God heal all so that we could live at least without the pain of physical suffering like this? And my answer is, 'Yes, He could.' But that also would not be perfect Love. And His Love is perfect. The Hand of God's will is even in sickness, through which He calls our hearts deeper to Himself. He uses such suffering (as He uses the sufferings caused by others' sins) to open our hearts – to give us a thirst and need for Him. If our hearts did not encounter situations of weakness—such that sickness brings to us—we would quickly forget God. A person must thirst in order to be open enough to receive the depths of Love's drink that the Cross offers. Jesus suffered thirst on the Cross to open us—and He calls us to meet Him in that as well. Nothing in life is coincidental. All is gift. When we live such fiat as Jesus did especially on the Cross, we receive deep peace through His Blood pouring from our wounds united to His Own. Our Shepherd is good. He takes most darkness, temptations, pain and sin upon Himself. And He enters into ours in order to teach us Love in the midst of all. Jesus did come to enter into suffering to heal us *in* it. He did enter into suffering to redeem it to give us strength and blessing, to teach us *Love* in the midst of it. In that, only in Love in the midst of the Cross, are we molded and fired like unto Him. He did not want us to be alone and so He came to enter the depths of aloneness and abandonment so that when these gifts kiss our lives we find Him and from Him the capacity to Love. And these gifts will come – in concrete ways. Our patience will be tried by trying situations and people. And we will succeed in Love, conquer sin in Love with Jesus, if we look to Him in trials and not to ourselves, not at the situations themselves. We must let Him take us deeper to find His Beauty present in all– and if He shows to us His crucified Beauty, we will be more blessed than all!

Jesus did not stare at His nails on the Cross and we should not look at those situations that crucify us. He did not look at Himself, feeling sorry or pity for Himself, and so we should imitate Him in that. If He would have looked at Himself, the Cross would have crushed Him. For Crucifixion without an answer of supreme Love is hell. On the Cross, Jesus looked in faith, in fiat obedience unto death, in trust upon the Love of the Father from which He was blinded. He looked in hope. We too, on the Cross, should not look at the nails of our lives or at ourselves but we should look at Him, our Beloved Christ Crucified, who makes visible the Love of the Father. We have something Jesus did not on the Cross – we have the Father's Love made visible in His Son, Crucified.

The nails will be real in our lives, in our hearts, just as they are real for Jesus Crucified. But the answer of Love will also be real as we receive the strength we need from Jesus to act as He did in forgiveness, surrender and obedience. Our words of kindness to those who persecute us will bring peace to our hearts and comfort to Jesus as real as His image left on Veronica's cloth. His answer and gift to us is His image imprinted upon us. The cloth we give is our hearts from which come all thoughts, words and actions. In always seeing the crosses in our lives as places of encounter with Jesus, and in always answering in Love, we will be able to give drink to His weary Heart. From the desert of the Cross Jesus said, *'I thirst.'* May we quench His thirst for love by being with Him in all situations, peoples and states of heart He may give to us and by always answering Him in Love, for Love, by Love.

VI

And Jesus was Silent

There are many different types of silences: silences full of self, silences of indifference and silences bursting full of Love. Jesus' silence on the Cross was a deafening silence. It was not empty, but a silence full of Love, of obedient Love. His silent reception and gentle response to all the abuse and torture thrown upon Him silenced His persecutors. Even as Pilate questioned Him, it is written that, *"He did not answer him one word, so that the governor was greatly amazed."* (Mt 27: 14) Jesus' silence in His Passion was one of Love for those who sinned against Him. His silence on the Cross was one of listening, expecting, waiting, hoping and trusting His Father. It was a silence of reception – of receiving all as a deep gift of the Father's Love. Yes! Even in the horror of the Cross, Jesus saw it was a gift of His Father's Merciful Love, for Jesus saw everything in truth. And the truth was that His pain was the means of Salvation for the whole universe. To be held captive by silence is to be held captive by Love. Jesus was silent because His focus was on the Father's Love carrying Him in suffering. Jesus' silence spoke louder than words. His silence spoke of His trust in His Father and in surrender to His Father's will. If Jesus had spoken many words during His Passion, they may have been rejected, ignored, mocked and misunderstood. But Jesus' silence on the Cross made room for the Holy Spirit to hiddenly, mysteriously enter in and begin to unlock hearts to receive their redemption. In silence Jesus did not complain against the Father and did not defend Himself. No, in silence He lived a deep childlike trust knowing and believing even in the empty darkness that His Father was with Him and that Love would conquer death. All of hell was unleashed against Jesus on the Cross, but His silence drew attention away from the hatred and temptation and drew the gaze of hearts to the Father and His Love. Yes, Jesus did speak several times from the Cross—Scripture records seven different 'words'; yet, Jesus did not speak any of these words on His Own. No, the whole time Jesus was on the Cross He was listening, receiving deep to His Heart the Father's will and answering with obedient Love. And so, each of His words from the Cross was a response in union with the Holy Spirit of Love. He spoke only when Love called Him to. Otherwise, He hung waiting for, trusting in His Father's invisible, intangible, silent Love. This is Fiat.

We must Love with Jesus' depth of silence, His depth of listening in our piece of His Cross as well. We are called also to silence, not only of words, but of heart, of mind, of emotions and memory; silence of fears and of desires. This is done by a great movement of the Holy Spirit's Love in us, consuming each of our faculties. This silence is not empty, but full of trustful Love. This silence waits in trust for a glance, a word, a breath of the Beloved. Jesus was attentive to His Father in silent Love. In imitating Him in this, we can become like Him. Our hearts can be consumed in Love, a Love beyond words and a Love able to forgive and offer great mercy to all others in the midst of our crosses. This is what it means to be crucified with Christ – to be tested by Love. And in attentive, obedient surrender to the Father, His Love can work and do all in us, for us, through us. Amen. Jesus teaches us that *a silent heart is a martyred heart, a heart martyred by loving attentiveness to her Beloved.*

Listening naturally means selection – a choice which has its root in the will. If we listen to one person, we automatically tune out and choose to not listen to other noises or to our thoughts. When Jesus was on the Cross, He did not listen to those mocking Him, to the devil tempting Him, or to self-pity. Jesus did not listen to the world or to His Own mind's or body's sufferings. No, from the Cross Jesus listened to the Father – even though His Father seemed far. He listened in faith, believing His Father's silent, deep Love spoke and led Him. He lost Himself in listening in Love to the Father – and in this He naturally turned from the world and the devil screaming at Him. In our lives, we must allow Jesus to not only live in us, but to listen in us. This includes turning our attention from the world's ideas, (which are often fabricated images) and even from ourselves. In putting our attention on Jesus, united with Jesus listening in us, our hearts can be opened to great mysteries of the Father's Love even in the midst of a loud, confusing world. His Love can fill and silence our thoughts, emotions, body and heart if we make room for Him, invite Him, wait for Him and rejoice in Him when we are aware of His presence. When we listen, what we may hear is silence, but in listening to silence we listen to the mysterious work of the Holy Spirit; and in such loving attention to Him, He is able to open, fill, guide and transform us. In looking and listening to Jesus' Love in the presence of the Holy Spirit in our crosses, Jesus can fill us with peace.

Jesus, come and listen in us. Help Your Love consume all of our faculties, every part of our beings, each relationship we have, every aspect of our lives. Amen.

VII

Littleness and the Cross

Like a weaned child on its mother's lap,
so is my soul within me... (Psalm 131:2b)

'*Amen, I say to you, unless you turn and*
become like children, you will not enter the
kingdom of heaven.' (Mt 18:3) You cannot
come to Jesus on the Cross with a mask. For
Jesus on the Cross shows us truth – the truth
of our sins, the truth of our dignity and the
truth of His Love. You must come to Him
pure and naked, just as you are deep inside
yourself, like a weak, little child, in order to
receive all the gifts He wishes to share from
His Crucified Love. To be with Jesus in the
life of His Cross it is absolutely necessary to
be little. Because the life of His Cross is so

great, we need His strength, Love, obedience, faith and hope in order to endure it. And we can only be filled with these gifts if we are first empty of ourselves. In the Night of the Cross we must be carried by God, for it is dark and we are blind and confused. To be carried by God means to not walk ourselves – to surrender and to trust. It means to allow Him to lift us to Himself and to direct our path. The littlest sheep are the ones that the Good Pastor carries. And these littlest sheep are closest, in His arms, to His Heart. We must be the littlest sheep, trusting our Shepherd and resting on His Heart. In this sort of surrender, He Himself can do many miracles of grace and Love in us and through us.

Our Lord is a great Gentleman. He does not force His way into anyone's heart. He respects the great gift of freedom, which He endowed each of us with because He so greatly respects our capability to love. We must be little, willing to let Him open us, undress us, heal us, fill us. Yes, it is His work even to make us little, but we must give Him our hearts with a little 'yes' allowing Him to fill us with His Love. It is His gift, but we must want to receive it.

God is almighty. We are not. But what Christ shows us on the Cross is that when we give the Father our nothingness in obedience –when we crucify our desires and place our little selves before Him in Fiat– He can do great things in us. He can live great Love in us. These things may not be visible, yet they can change the world. He can fill our mundane everyday lives with His divine Love and this gives Him glory and can profoundly affect the world. All He needs is our 'yes'. Jesus teaches us this from the Cross. In His Crucifixion He was still, for His hands and feet were bound with nails, and He was almost completely silent. In worldly eyes, He was nothing and did nothing. But in the eyes of the Father, He did everything and therefore redeemed the world. This everything that He did was obedience and

Love. In His obedience and Love in the Cross, God the Almighty could do all. It is true that in our sinful nature we are too weak to obey and love as perfectly as Jesus, yet this is what we are called to do. And the means of doing this seemingly impossible task of perfect obedience and Love, even in the Crucifixion, is littleness and complete surrender of ourselves to the Hands, Heart and will of Jesus Crucified. When we empty ourselves before Him in humility (and humility is truth: the truth about God and the truth about us), then He can fill us with all we need and carry us, resting in His Heart, through the storm of the Cross. St. Paul writes in His Letter to the Colossians that Jesus gives us *'peace by the blood of His Cross'.* (Col 1:20) And Jesus invites us to live deeply that peace, even in the midst of all sorts of tribulations. He offers us this peace by His Presence with us, His grace with us in all we encounter in life. His presence is bigger than any problem or tragedy in our life, for *'He is greater than our hearts...'* (1 John 3:20b)

Jesus invites us to sleep in the boat with Him, during the storm. In Matthew's Gospel the disciples question Jesus as they feared for their lives in the boat in the storm and all the while Jesus slept. Jesus answers them saying, *'Why are you terrified, O you of little faith?'* (Mt 8:26) The difference between the disciples and Jesus in that situation is the key to how Jesus suffered in the Cross. The disciples looked at the storm and worried about themselves. They said, *'Lord, save us! We are perishing!'* (Mt 8:25) They were not concerned with Jesus as much as their own lives. But Jesus was not afraid. He looked not at the storm or His disciples' fear around Him. He looked at the Father, trusting Him as a little child trusts his parent. His eyes and Heart were with His Father in faith and Love and so He was so peaceful that He could rest, sleep, in the midst of all. In the Cross Jesus suffered terribly, but He did not look at the storm or His sufferings. He looked trustingly to the Father, with the faith and obedience of His Heart, even when it seemed His Father was gone. And this carried Him through all. Yes, He cried, *'My God, My God, why have you forsaken Me?'* (Mt 27:46) But the end of this Psalm, which Jesus' Heart prayed, contains great hope. The depths of His Heart rested in the will of the Father and His unseen, unfelt, but believed in Love. In this, Jesus found *'peace by the blood of His Cross.'* If we can, like a child, watch Him in the midst of our suffering, He can give us this peace as well. He desires to give us this gift – we simply must go naked before Him and ask.

We can learn much from babies. A little baby sleeps a lot, not worrying about his life, but trusting completely in his parents. When he is awake his eyes are on his mother, watching her move throughout the room. If she is not visible, he often sits and rests. Sometimes he cries, and when his mother takes him in her arms, he is calm. His life is being with her. This simplicity of a child is holy. A baby is innocent, living a life of receiving what he needs from those who care for him – nothing more. And this is how God created us to live with Him, as children receiving all we need and living in trust. When God created Adam and Eve this is how they lived with Him in Eden. The Bible tells us that God gave them everything on earth at their disposal. But Adam and Eve sinned, grasping at knowledge. They did not want to live a simple life of trust in God. They disobeyed because they stepped out of trusting their Father and His Love. When Jesus came, He lived the perfect trust-relationship with His Father that God intended for humans in the beginning. He taught us in Matthew 6:25-34 that we should live as God's little children, seeking Him and trusting Him with the rest of our lives. This littleness allows us to be empty of ourselves and allows for God to give us all the great gifts He desires. It allows for Him to give us the grace we need in our cross to find union with Jesus. Such trust allows us to live Psalm 131 in the midst of the Cross. It is to pray, in the midst of our darkness and suffering, the prayer: *'Lord, my heart is not proud; nor are my eyes haughty. I do not busy myself with great matters, with things too sublime for me. Rather, I have stilled my soul, hushed it like a weaned child. Like a weaned child on his mother's lap, so is my soul within me. Israel, hope in the Lord, now and forever.'* (Ps 131)

A child's life is full of hope. If we can be little with Jesus in our lives crucified with Him, He can fill us with great hope of Resurrection, of hope in the true reality of our eternal life with Him to come.

What is this littleness that Jesus calls us to live with Him in the Cross? Jesus shows us that ***littleness is purity of heart – it is the humility of Truth of who you are before God. It is having a soft, docile heart in the Hands of your Father, which He will mold, shape, guide. It is to have nothing of your***

58

own, but everything from Him, in Him. It is to have every need of yours provided for by Him before you know there is a need. It is not to worry, or even think too much about yourself or life itself – simply to live in trust. It is to not be afraid or shy in His Arms, before His Face, even if you are naked – for you came forth from His Heart in Love, were formed by His Hands and He will clothe you. It is to have a ready, listening heart, a very obedient heart. It is to obey His every desire without thinking, simply rejoicing in His Love, desiring to please Him and trusting that He knows, wants and will give to you what is best. Littleness is to decide nothing on your own, but to ask His permission for all. It is to look to Him alone for comfort and help in suffering – only He can satisfy your heart. It is to never be afraid – for when you are with such a strong Person Who so dearly loves you, nothing can go wrong. He protects, He guides, He gives, He loves. It is to do all just to please Him – eat what He wants, play what He wants. It is to forget yourself in Him. It is to sleep calmly on His Chest during a storm. It is faith; it is trust; it is sincerity and truth; it is simple, free love.

VIII

Spousalship and the Cross

Love desires to be with the Beloved. Jesus Himself gives us the perfect example of this in His relationship with His Father. Jesus says in John 14:11, *'Believe Me that I am in the Father and the Father is in Me.'* And as we are His beloved, He invites us to always be with Him. *'As the Father loves Me, so I also love you. Remain in My love.'* (Jn 15:9) True love always seeks to be with the object of his love. And if the beloved suffers, he desires to not only be with him as he suffers, but to take that suffering on himself. This is what Jesus did for us on the Cross. This is how He loved – He emptied Himself so that He could not only be with us in our sufferings, but also so that He could take our sufferings upon Himself. And this is the type of union He is inviting us to enter into with Him on the

Cross. In marriage this desire of perfect faithful union, regardless of the circumstances, is seen in the vows exchanged by husband and wife. They promise to love each other in good times and bad, in riches and poverty, in sickness and in health. This is the sort of love we should always live with Jesus. We should love our dear Savior so much that we desire to be with Him not only in joy, but also in His sufferings, especially in His sufferings when He most needs us. We should desire to not only be with Him, but to share with Him in these sufferings so that He is not alone. Love should be the force that carries us through our crosses in life –love for Jesus, Who is allowing us to share a little with Him in all He endured to save us and all of humanity.

Our crosses are our places of union with our Beloved Jesus. They are kisses of His wounds in our life. When a man and wife come together in holy marital love, they are naked. They desire for nothing to come between perfect union of their bodies and of their souls. Jesus comes to each one of us like this, in deep Marital Love, in crucified Love. The Cross is our nuptial bed. Our wounds uncovered meet with His in this dark night of marital joy. He becomes one with us as He takes our wounds into His Own Body and Soul, and as He shares with us a taste of the bitter cup He drank from the Father. He suffered to heal us. When we accept suffering in Love, we can not only receive this healing, but we can also soothe His pain. Our Love is a dialog. He gives, we receive. We give, He receives. He became poor to make us rich— rich in Love and rich in eternal life in His Heavenly Kingdom. When we become poor for Him, with Him, He can fill us with all His gifts here on earth, and the great gift of life eternal with Him. This is our hope in the Cross –the hope of deep union with our merciful Savior– He Who suffered more than any other man on earth. This is our hope in the Cross, that the *'Man of Sorrows'* (Is 53) may become our Spouse of Love.

Look how Jesus loved us in the Cross. Look how He proposed to us, inviting us to enter into a marriage of deep Spousal Love with Him. He suffered terribly and laid down His life – He gave us all in order to open us to receive the gift of Himself. He became covered in blood, to wash our tears away. Perfect union with Christ must take place on the road of Calvary, for this is the path which made Him one with us. When a husband and wife are married, a man takes her into his home; his family is her family; his food is her food; his bed is her bed; his life is her life. When Jesus takes a soul spousally to Himself, He takes her into His bed of the Cross; she eats of His food of bitter wounds with Him; she shares in His life of darkness, loneliness and abandon. Yet, His family becomes hers – His heavenly Father is her Father; His kingdom of Heaven is her Kingdom for eternity. They share Crosses, and they share crowns. Deeper than the union of a human man and wife, the soul is one with her Beloved Lord. This union of Crucified Love is full of joy, for with each little suffering that we embrace in fiat, we are that much more deeply united with Him – one with the Son of God! There is no greater joy than that.

As we receive the kiss of Jesus' wounds in our lives, let our hearts rejoice that He loves us enough to share the deepest part of His Love with us – His suffering Love. And may we not be frightened by our sufferings – external or internal– for we have a good Husband Who cares for us more than we could understand. As Christ became one body with us in the Incarnation and by taking our sins and sufferings on Himself, as He unites one with us in His body and Heart's gift in the Eucharist, so we too become one body with Him in sharing in His Cross. He gives His body to us in the Eucharist, and we give Him our body to be one with His. In this union is such sweet peace and joy, even if there is suffering or loss involved, because in this union with Jesus we have gained that which we were created for: a perfect Love union with the Father. He, our perfect Spouse, places in our hearts His Love union with the Father. Yes, He gives us all of this if we only say 'yes' in abandon to His will.

St. Paul beautifully writes about Jesus' Marital Love for us from the Cross, *"Husbands, love your wives, even as Christ loved the church and handed himself over for her to sanctify her, cleansing her by the bath of water with the word, that he might present to himself the church in splendor, without spot or wrinkle or any such thing, that she might be holy and without blemish. So also husbands should love their wives as their own bodies. He who loves his wife loves himself. For no one hates his own flesh but rather nourishes and cherishes it, even as Christ does the church, because we are members of his body. 'For this reason a man shall leave his father and his mother and be joined to his*

wife, and the two shall become one flesh.'
This is a great mystery, but I speak in
reference to Christ and the church."
(Ephesians 5:22-32)

Jesus loves us as a Spouse. May we open our hearts in naked surrender before Him to receive this saving Love and allow it to transform our lives. May we pray with every beat of our hearts, "Maranatha! Come, Lord Jesus! "

IX

Mary of Calvary

"Standing by the Cross of Jesus was His Mother." (Jn 19:25)

Mary of Calvary. What was Her role in the life of Her Son's crucified Love? She stood at the foot of the Cross. And in this She fiated with Him. She stood, as a sign of faith that God's redemption of humanity was stronger than death. She stood by in hope, the hope of giving Her Son comfort in His affliction and in hope of the Resurrection, of the conquering of Love. She stood by in Love, absorbing the awe of Her Son's merciful Love and keeping Her own heart open in abandon with Him so that the Love She received She could offer back to Him. Mary could not take the suffering from Jesus on Calvary, and even if She could have I do not believe She would have. She would not have interfered in God's divine plan of Love and Salvation. Her standing by the Cross was not consent to Jesus' suffering in apathy, but consent deep in Her will to all Her Son and Her Father had willed. It was not a desire to see Her Son suffer, but a desire for eternal redemption bigger than this life's suffering. It was the desire for the conquering of Love.

Even if Jesus was surrounded by blackness and terror, His Mother's presence had to have held a little light for Him, even if He did not always see Her. Mary stood at the foot of Her Son's Cross with a fiat, the same fiat that She had given 33 years before when the angel had asked Her to be His mother. She raised Jesus in an atmosphere of fiat, in a home full of loving abandonment to the will of the Beloved Father. She raised Him to be obedient. She raised Him to always follow the call of Love. Whether Jesus would have embraced the Cross without the beautiful upbringing His mother gave Him is not the question, for He came to earth to redeem man and did not 'need' to learn from His Mother to do this. Yet Her upbringing of Him was a cultivating of Her heart – a preparation for His death in a way; Her upbringing of Him intertwined their Hearts in one fiat, so that in His Passion She would have the courage to stand by His Cross, Her heart crucified as She watched Him suffer, fiating with Him. Her presence had to be deep consolation, even if not to His emotions, to His will that knew She was there. Mary stood by Jesus' Cross not only as He lived and suffered there, but even after He had died. She must have felt at that moment deep union with Her Son's interior sufferings of abandonment by the Father on the Cross, yet She did not pity Herself in this aching of Her heart. No, She must have drawn deep strength and hope from Her Son's fiat; She must have seen how He embraced the Cross in such hopeful Love that She did not doubt that His death was the end. Maybe She did not know the details of His Resurrection, but She, in great faith, believed God's salvific Love and plan was greater than the rejected Love and death that Her Son suffered.

And so what is Mary's role in our lives, as we are called to share in Crucified Love with Her Son? It is the same. Just as Mary stood at the foot of Jesus' Cross, She stands at the foot of ours. Just as She kept Her eyes and heart on the hope of the Resurrection and conquering of Love in Jesus' Passion, so too will She hold the Light of Hope in the strength of God's Love and the gift of Life eternal in our night. She is our Lamp of hope and Love. In the darkest of our nights, knowing of Her presence, love and faithfulness is an inconceivable consolation to our hearts. She lived in darkness with Jesus and She will live with us. She said fiat in Her heart with Jesus, and She will say fiat with us. Mary was Jesus' Mother and He gave Her to us. As we join one with Him on the Cross in Spousal Love, our relationship with Her (the Mother of our Crucified Spouse) intensifies. She is our Mother too. Just as She raised Jesus in an atmosphere of Love, of fiat and of obedience to the Father, She will be our Mother and teacher too. Just as Jesus looked on Her from the Cross, so too can we. Her heart, so pure, is our Light. For the Light and fullness of God's Love reigns in Her pure heart full of fiat. Just as Mary did not take Her Son's suffering away, neither will She take ours. For this suffering is our means of union with Her Son, is a kiss of Love from the Father to make us images of His Son in Love. Yet, Her presence can give us hope, as we know She prays for us. When it is darkest and we cannot see or feel Her Motherly care, we know She stands by us. We know She prays for us. And even if we believe that we cannot endure any longer, She believes for us, for She stood at the foot of Her Son's Cross and has seen the power of God's grace and merciful

Love. When things are very bleak, and we cannot even picture Her face, we must say Her name over and over – 'Mary, Mary, Mary, Come, Help me.' We know that She is with God; we know that She loves, cares and prays for us; and we know that Her prayer is powerful. Just as the Mother never abandoned Her Son, She will never abandon us, Her little children and His beloved ones. May Her faithfulness help us to be faithful. May Her Son's Love help us to always fiat in faith with Her. Amen. Alleluia.

PART TWO

For your prayerful meditation:
Reflections on Jesus' Way of the Cross
and Resurrection

X

Jesus' Passion, Cross, and Death

1) Jesus Gives Himself to Us in His Gift of the Eucharist

"Jesus took bread, said the blessing, broke it, and giving it to his disciples said, 'Take and eat; this is my body.' Then he took a cup, gave thanks, and gave it to them, saying, 'Drink from it, all of you, for this is my blood of the covenant, which will be shed on behalf of many for the forgiveness of sins." Mt 26:26-28

"When he had said this, Jesus was deeply troubled and testified, 'Amen, Amen I say to you, one of you will betray me.'" Jn 13:21

"One of his disciples, the one whom Jesus loved, was reclining at Jesus' side." Jn 13:23

"I am the bread of life; whoever comes to me will never hunger, and whoever believes in me will never thirst." Jn 6:35

"I am the living bread that came down from heaven; whoever eats this bread will live forever; and the bread that I will give is my flesh for the life of the world. Amen, Amen I say to you, unless you eat of the flesh of the Son of Man and drink his blood, you do not have life within you. Whoever eats my flesh and drinks my blood has eternal life, and I will raise him on the last day. For my flesh is true food, and my blood is true drink. Whoever eats my flesh and drinks my blood remains in me, and I in him." Jn 6:51, 53-56

Jesus, **"What does it mean to share a cup? It is a sign of intimacy between people, and a sign of trust. As two people consume** the same substance, they are united in a way. Yet how more deeply intimate is it when a mother nurses her child? She shares with her baby a food which is her very self. Yet in the Eucharistic food which I shared with My disciples, I gave much more than simply union through our sharing one bread and one cup, even if the food I gave them was Myself. In the Eucharist I gave them My body and blood which would be shed for them, for the forgiveness of sins. The Eucharist would have had little meaning without My Cross. I gave My body as a gift to be wounded by them so that I could heal them. I gave all of My Love to be rejected and abandoned by their weakness in order to give them strength. I called them to be one with Me in the Eucharist, to the shedding of their own blood with Me, for Me, in Love. The union I called them into with Me, and which I call you into with Me, is a living union of total self-emptying in gift for the Beloved. It is a union I call you to enter into with Me as I consume you in My covenant of Love; and it is a union I call you to enter in and live with Me on the Cross, as we are wounded together for Love of your brothers and sisters in the world. The Love I place within you in the Eucharist is a broken Love, a crucified Love; a Love which loves so much that it is even willing to be deeply hurt simply for the sake of Love. The covenant I draw you into with Me on the Cross, in the Eucharist, is a covenant of Love that lives in you. You die with Me, to Me, in Me as you receive My Eucharist Body and Blood, and I –your Beloved Spouse –come to live My life in you.

All you need to live the life of the Cross to which I have called you, you received the first time you received Me in the Eucharist. There was your strength, all the clarity, grace, answers you needed for your life now. And each time you receive Me in the Eucharist, I renew My covenant of Love with you –offering you a Love so great that it is willing to be deeply wounded. Yet My Eucharist can live always in you, as you fiat to My Cross and receive deeply to your heart My crucified life and Love within you. My crucified Love is a Eucharistic Love—a Love that unites, heals and strengthens. And My Cross lives in My Eucharistic Heart. Open yourself up to live My Eucharistic Crucified Love with Me, daily. And I bless you in My Love. Amen."

2) Jesus Prays and Suffers in the Garden

"He said to them, 'My soul is sorrowful even to death. Remain here and keep watch with Me.' He advanced a little and fell prostrate in prayer, saying, 'My Father, if it is possible, let this cup pass from Me; yet not as I will, but as you will.'" Mt 26:38-39

"And to strengthen him an angel from heaven appeared to him. He was in such agony and he prayed so fervently that his sweat became like drops of blood falling on the ground." Lk 22:43-44

"I am troubled now. Yet what should I say? 'Father save me from this hour?' But it was for this purpose that I came to this hour." Jn 12:27

Jesus, "I was so alone that night in the garden. The depth of My loneliness is something I cannot describe to you in words. It is just something you shall know with Me, as I open up this mystery of suffering within you. My loneliness consumed every part of My Being. I suffered as a human, so abandoned and misunderstood by My friends. I suffered as the Divine Son, for although My Father sent His angel to comfort Me, I already could not see His shining Face as the darkness of the Cross' Night already had begun to fill Me. I suffered as Savior, taking the great loneliness of sinners separated from My Father on Myself –a loneliness which seemed to be insatiable as their hearts were so closed to receiving My blood's forgiveness and healing Love. And I suffered as Son, for I knew the sufferings My Mother would endure, and I knew Her desire to comfort Me which She could not realize. Yes, I suffered loneliness for Her and all My little just ones in this world. I suffered as Spouse, for My Bride the Church and all Her members which would be misunderstood, abandoned and rejected on account of Me. I suffered in many other ways as well. I suffered disgust of all the most evil and inhumane, hideous sins that mankind had or would commit. I especially suffered for My littlest ones, the tender-hearted, who would endure such cruelty. I suffered the guilt of all mankind for their sins, as I saw what I would embrace by taking their sins upon Me on the Cross. I suffered temptations which also repulsed

Me as they overcame Me; I saw so much, so deep, into the darkness that humanity had invited to reign in My Father's good world through sin. And most of all what saddened Me was I saw so many of My children who were lost, who would reject the healing gift of My Love and forgiveness. I saw all those who would stray so far from Me and My Father through no fault of their own – simply because they did not know the truth. They are victims with Me, although they do not know Me. And I need people in My Church to carry My blood and crucified Love –My Love wounded open for them – to them. I saw all the hatred, darkness and cruelty that I would have to endure and although My Heart fiated to My Father's will in all of it, My body, My senses, My emotions and My mind seemed to panic with such fear that blood was forced through My pores, dripping to the ground. Yet, My sweat of blood was not only a sign of My distress –it was a sign of My great

Love as well. My Heart was filled with a great Love for all My people as they passed before the eyes of My Heart. I was tempted that all My great suffering would not even help them, and My Heart fought hard to fiat, to believe, to trust and to love even more. And My Heart, overcoming all My other senses, loved so greatly that she sent forth her blood as a kiss to the world –as a promise that she would give and shed all, every last drop, for those I loved. My blood was not wasted on the ground that night. No, it spoke very loudly through all the ages that I, the Savior of the world, loved My children and would give all I was unto death for the forgiveness of their sins and to restore them to My Father. Yes, My blood on the ground that night responded to all the evil tempting Me that My Love would conquer. I was very weak and tired from My intense prayer, yet My Father sent an angel of His Love to strengthen Me. He would not ask more of Me than I was physically able to do for Him. The angel strengthened My body, so it could contain all the love rushing from My Heart.

You do not have to spend the night in such intense prayer as I did, for I have already done that for you. But you can open your heart, your life, and allow Me to pray for you in My prayer of Gethsemane within you. You will not suffer similar to Me, you will allow Me to suffer within you. That is a big difference. You will not suffer your own Cross, but instead you can allow My Body, My Heart, My Spirit and My Love to suffer in you. In this, My suffering in you, I can heal and save the world. I already suffered all and died for the salvation of all. Yet by your fiat, you will make that suffering visible to them so that they may know it, fall in love with it and receive all the graces I wish to give them from it. More importantly, by allowing Me to share all this suffering within you, we will be united deeply in it. And this I know you desire deeply as My spouse. My suffering in you will bear fruit to help the whole world; but even if it didn't, your union to Me in it would be enough fruit to make all I have done in you 'worth it'. For I have saved your soul by the path of Love Crucified in your life. Now rest, and receive all I give you deep into your heart, treasuring it in love. Amen.

And yes, I bless you in your work of resting love."

3) Betrayal of Jesus

"Jesus, knowing everything that was going to happen to him, went out and said to them, 'Whom are you looking for?' They answered him, 'Jesus the Nazorean.' He said to them, 'I am.' Judas his betrayer was also with them. When he said 'I am' they turned away and fell to the ground." Jn18:4-6

"While he was still speaking, Judas, one of the Twelve, arrived, accompanied by a large crowd, with swords and clubs, who had come from the chief priests and the elders of the people. His betrayer had arranged a sign with them, saying, 'The man I shall kiss is the one; arrest him.' Immediately he went over to Jesus and said, 'Hail Rabbai!' and he kissed him. Jesus answered him, 'Friend, do what you have come for.'" Mt 26:47-50

"Jesus said to Peter, 'Put your sword into its scabbard. Shall I not drink the cup that the Father gave me?'" Jn 18:11

Jesus, **"A kiss is a deep sign of affection. And so when My beloved disciple used this sign of love to betray Me, My Heart grieved deeply –not for Myself, but for My friend who had allowed deceit to so deeply overpower his soul. My crucifixion was not Judas' fault, as the Jews had planned to kill Me for quite some time. Yet his betrayal of**

Me was his sin, a sin that gripped his conscience so tightly that it cost him his own life. How I wished his pride would have allowed him to be sorry, admitting his fault, and receiving My forgiving and healing Love. How I yearned to guide him to the foot of My Cross with John, to show him how much I loved him and to show the world how great is My forgiveness. But he would not allow Me to love him in this way, and that grieved My Heart more than anything. I, as Savior, would have desired for him to stand side by side John at the foot of My Cross in repentance. Do not ever think that I despised Judas for what he did. No, I always loved My persecutors, and especially this brother of Mine. My greatest suffering in his betrayal was not because My Love was rejected and this hurt Me. No, My greatest suffering was that in Judas' weakness and pride he rejected My Love and thus condemned himself. I will not tell you what happened to Judas' soul, yet I will tell you that it is very hard for My Love to save a person who condemns themselves – who does not feel capable of receiving My forgiveness, or maybe does not want it. These darkest souls I pity the most. And I ask you to pity them with Me. On that dark night I knew the path that lay before Me, and My Father gave Me the strength to walk forward embracing it, His will, in Love. Yet My soul was mostly grieved by all My brothers standing before Me in that moment, so overtaken by the devil's lies and hatred that they could not see the Truth of My Love. Yet I loved these men deeply, and guarded My every word and step, so that maybe through their persecution of Me they might see their wrong and receive My forgiving Love. I died for Love of them, to save them each from eternal damnation. I ask you to love your persecutors –those who persecute My life and Love within you, with the same strength of gentle Love I showed Judas that night.

As I said, Judas did not cause My death himself. And neither did the Jews that so desired it, even planned it. I freely laid down My life in Love, allowing the sins of the entire world to crush Me, kill Me. I allowed this so that My Love could triumph and heal those who killed Me. And so I ask you to please allow My forgiveness to live that deeply in you. I ask you to dearly love and weep for those who crucify Me in you. And may your tears of My forgiving Love change their hearts and lead to their salvation as well. I bless you with My broken Heart, from whence you receive the strength, humility and love you need to live My merciful Love. Amen."

4) The Trials of Jesus

"Though he was harshly treated, he submitted and opened not his mouth; like a lamb led to the slaughter or a sheep before the shearers, he was silent and opened not his mouth." Is 53,7

"Some began to spit on him. They blindfolded him and struck him and said to him, 'Prophesy!' And the guards greeted him with blows." Mk14:65

"But Jesus was silent." Mt 26:63

"Then the high priest said to him, 'I order you to tell us under oath before the living God whether you are the Messiah, the Son of God.' Jesus said to him in reply, 'You have said so, but I tell you: From now on you will see 'the Son of Man' seated at the right hand of the power and coming on the clouds of heaven.'" Mt 26:63-4

"He questioned him, 'Are you the King of the Jews?' Jesus said, 'You say so.'" Mt 27:11

"But he did not answer him one word, so that the governor was greatly amazed." Mt 27:14

"They said, 'If you are the Messiah, tell us.' But he replied to them, 'If I tell you, you will not believe, and if I question, you will not respond...'" Lk 22:67

"He questioned him at length, but he gave him no answer." Lk 23:9

"The high priest questioned Jesus about his disciples and about his doctrine. Jesus answered him, 'I have spoken publicly to the world. I have always taught in a synagogue or in the temple area where all the Jews gather, and in secret I have said nothing. Why ask Me? Ask those who heard Me what I said to them. They know what I said.' When he had said this, one of the temple guards standing there struck Jesus and said, 'Is this the way you answer the high priest?' Jesus answered them, 'If I have spoken wrongly testify to the wrong; but if I have spoken rightly, why do you strike Me?'" Jn 18:19-23

"Pilate said to Jesus, 'Where are you from?' Jesus did not answer him. So Pilate said to him, 'Do you not speak to me? Do you not know that I have power to release you and I have power to crucify you?' Jesus answered him, 'You would have no power over me if it had not been given to you from above. For this reason the one who handed me over to you has the greater sin.'" Jn 19:9-11

"So Pilate went back into the Praetorium and summoned Jesus and said to him, 'Are you the King of the Jews?' Jesus answered, 'Do you say this on your own or have others told you about me?; Pilate answered, 'I am not a Jew, am I? Your own nation and priests handed you over to me. What have you done?' Jesus answered, 'My kingdom does not belong to this world. If My kingdom did

belong to this world, My attendants would be fighting to keep Me from being handed over to the Jews. But as it is, My kingdom is not here.' So Pilate said to him, 'So you are a king?' Jesus answered, 'You say I am a king. For this I was born and for this I came into the world, to testify to the truth. Everyone who belongs to the truth listens to My voice.'"
Jn 18:33-37

Jesus, "**My trials were something I suffered deeply within Myself. This was the time particularly of My suffering in relationships. I knew the hearts before Me –those who questioned and those who watched, and I desired more than anything to witness to them the innocence of Truth. I knew that My death was inevitable; it had already been agreed upon by My Father and I in order to save mankind. Yet the purpose of the trials, in addition to saddening My human Heart causing Me to suffer all the more, was for those who questioned Me. I**

could have answered them exactly as they
desired so that they could go ahead with
their plan to put Me to death. But I waited,
in silence, calling with My silent, still Love
for their hearts to be opened, broken of
pride, so that My Truth could enter. I had
to suffer for all people and in all times in
My Passion, and so I did not want to
neglect the sufferings of those under trial
unjustly –those accused, those who would
be tangled in evil's deceitful questions. I
wanted to suffer patiently for those who felt
they endured their trials alone. I wanted to
drink the full cup that My Father offered
allowing this suffering, too, to pierce My
soul. Those for whom I came to save
rejected Me. Their hearts did not
understand, for as they stepped out of Love,
they stepped away from My Wisdom that
could have helped their hearts grasp the
magnitude of the occurrences before them.

I want you to meditate on My ridiculed
Love. And I ask you to please enter these

words deeply –allow Me to open them and incarnate them in your life. For you are called to live and embrace your 'trials' with the same patient, silent, forgiving Love I did, only answering when the Spirit tells you to. And I bless you in your tried love, in My Love which will often be 'on trial' in your life. Amen"

TRIALS OF JESUS

Jesus, "I was the Word, and they rejected Me. I knew that they would more so reject My words, a reflection of Who I Am. I was the Truth, and they hated Me. How much more would they have hated and rejected My words of truth, mere reflections of Me? If they hated the tree, they would hate the fruit. No, I did not speak much under trial, persecution. I did not try to explain to them Who I was or My message of Love. Their hearts were not open, their hearts could not have received

My explanations. It was My mercy that kept My mouth closed. It was mercy, and not closed-heartedness, that kept Me silent. I loved My persecutors. I loved those who put Me on trial, who questioned Me, who beat Me. I knew that if I was silent, all they would hear would be the echo of their own heart's hatred, the echo of their sin. Silence is the language of the Holy Spirit, the Presence of My Love. The Holy Spirit needed to enter in to show them, convict them of their sin. Only after they saw their sin and repented, could they have received or understood My explanations, answers of truth. For truth is My presence. And My presence can only rest in hearts rid of sin. It pained Me greatly that I could not rest in their hearts in merciful Love, enlightening them, showing them truth, leading them to the Father. How I longed to bring My persecutors back home to My Father. But they did not want Him, and they did not want Me. In My silence, Who I was spoke louder than My words could have. My union with My Father carried Me through these moments. I allowed for Him to answer for Me, and His answer was His Love for them through Me. His answer to their questions would come, but in His time and way, not theirs. His answer would be My death, and My resurrection. Yet even this answer many could not receive until after I sent My Spirit at Pentecost –My Spirit would enlighten and cleanse their hearts of sin so that they could look back and receive the answer of 'Who I was' through My death and resurrection. And when I did answer their questions, I did not answer people so that they could necessarily understand. I answered to give witness to Truth. Truth brings Light, Love and Faith.

And so you as well will be put on trial many times. Never fear. I am with you in these times and offer you the grace to endure this through My own mysterious suffering of trials before My death. You are always to answer and witness to truth. And many will not understand the truth in you as they did not understand Me. That is because people desire to understand more than they love. You are to call them to love, and as they love through My Spirit of Love present within them, they will begin to understand. Understanding is a gift of the Holy Spirit. They must open their hearts to Him in love first. You are to listen to Him, the Holy Spirit, and keep your heart awake, resting always in Him –especially in these times of persecution or trial. Listen and obey. If He gives you words, speak. If He Himself desires to defend you, be silent and allow Him to speak to other's hearts. But always remain at rest with Him. Your life as well will witness to the truth. They may find their answers within the truth of My life and Love in your life. Yet if they reject your life –which imitates the Gospel and My commands therein –then they will also reject your words. Yet when their eyes are opened and they come to see My life within you and to accept it, they will also accept your words, My words to them through you –and My word to their lives through you will be Mercy. Live Mercy. Pray for mercy on yourself, the whole world, and those especially who persecute you. And My Mercy in you will touch and convert the world. This is the world's deepest need – Mercy –and I ask you to give it to them through your life, words and silence in union with Mine and My Father's will. If you obey Him, He will draw you to Himself through Me, and you will have nothing to fear. Rest with Me, and receive the graces I am giving you now to share in this suffering of Mine as well.

People love the sound of their own voices in the search of many questions more than they love Me. To understand is not wrong; reason is good. But people must love Me more than they seek to understand.

I am Truth; only through faith in Me, the Truth, will they receive the wisdom, understanding and answers of truth. They must love Me to receive Me. They must love truth, thirst for it, to receive it. It is not something man can grasp at and do alone. Everything is gift from My Father, even understanding, wisdom and truth. All comes through Me. "All things came to be through Him...(Jn 1:3)" They must seek Me, and not with selfish intentions, in order to be able to receive the answers they desire. Love them and help them love Me by your life of witness in union with Me. In this they will receive the answers to all their questions. They will receive Me, Truth Incarnate."

5) Peter Denies Jesus

"Then Jesus said to them, 'This night all of you will have your faith in me shaken, for it is written, 'I will strike the shepherd, and the sheep of the flock will be dispersed,' but after I have been raised up, I shall go before you to Galilee.' Peter said to him in reply, 'Though all may have their faith in you shaken, mine will never be.' Jesus said to him, 'Amen, I say to you, this very night before the cock crows, you will deny me three times.' Peter said to him, 'Even though I should have to die with you, I will not deny you.' And all the disciples spoke likewise." Mt 26:31-35

"He said to Peter, 'Simon, are you asleep? Could you not keep watch with Me for one hour? Watch and pray that you may not undergo the test. The spirit is willing, but the flesh is weak.'" Mk14:37b-38

"Now Peter was sitting outside in the courtyard one of the maids came over to him and said, 'You too were with Jesus the Galilean.' But he denied it in front of everyone, saying, 'I do not know what you are talking about!' As he went out to the gate, another girl saw him and said to those who were there, 'This man was with Jesus the Nazorean.' Again he denied it with an oath, 'I do not know the man!' A little later the bystanders came over and said to Peter, 'Surely you too are one of them; even your speech gives you away.' At that he began to curse and swear, 'I do not know the man.' And immediately the cock crowed. Then Peter remembered the word that Jesus had spoken, 'Before the cock crows you will deny me three times.' He went out and began to weep bitterly." Mt 26:69-75

"Peter said to him, 'Even though all should have their faith shaken, mine will not be. Then Jesus said to him, 'Amen I say to you, this very night before the cock crows twice you will deny me three times.' But he vehemently replied, 'Even though I should have to die with you, I will not deny you." Mk 14:29-31a

"While Peter was below in the courtyard, one of the high priest's maids came along. Seeing Peter warming himself, she looked intently at him and said, 'You too were with the Nazorean, Jesus.' But he denied it saying, 'I neither know nor understand what you are talking about.' So he went out into the outer court. Then the cock crowed. The maid saw him and began again to say to the bystanders, 'This man is one of them.' Once again he denied it. A little later the bystanders said to Peter once more, 'Surely you are one of them; for you too are a Galilean.' He began to curse and swear, 'I do not know this man about whom you are talking.' And immediately a cock crowed a second time. Then Peter remembered the word that Jesus had said to him, 'Before the cock crows twice, you will deny me three times.' He broke down and wept." Mk 14:66-72

"Simon, Simon, behold satan has demanded to sift all of you like wheat, but I have prayed that your own faith may not fail; and once you have turned back, you must strengthen your brothers. He said to him, 'Lord, I am prepared to go to prison and to die with you.' But he replied, 'I tell you, Peter, before the cock crows this day, you will deny three times that you know me.'" Lk 22:31-34

"After arresting him they led him away and took him into the house of the high priest; Peter was following at a distance. They lit a fire in the middle of the courtyard and sat around it, and Peter sat down with them. When a maid saw him seated in the light, she looked intently at him and said, 'This man too was with him.' But he denied it saying, 'Woman, I do not know him.' A short while later someone else saw him and said, 'You too are one of them,' but Peter answered, 'My friend, I am not.' About an hour later, still another insisted, 'Assuredly, this man too was with him, for he also is a Galilean.' But Peter said, 'My friend, I do not know what you are talking about.' Just as he was saying this, the cock crowed, AND THE LORD TURNED AND LOOKED AT PETER; and Peter remembered the words of the Lord, how he had said to him, 'Before the cock crows today, you will deny me three times.' He went out and began to weep bitterly. The men who held Jesus in custody were ridiculing and beating him." Lk 22:54-63

"Jesus said, 'My children, I will be with you only a little while longer. You will look for me, and as I told the Jews, 'Where I go you cannot come,' so now I say it to you. I give you a new commandment: love one another.' Simon Peter said to him, 'Master, where are you going?' Jesus answered him, 'Where I am going, you cannot follow me now, though you will follow later.' Peter said to him, 'Master, why can't I follow you now?' I will lay down my life for you.' Jesus answered, 'Will you lay down your life for me? Amen, Amen, I say to you, the cock will not crow before you deny me three times.'" Jn 13: 33-38

"Simon Peter and another disciple followed Jesus. Now the other disciple was known to the high priest, and he entered the courtyard of the high priest with Jesus. But Peter stood at the gate outside. So the other disciple, the acquaintance of the high priest, went out and spoke to the gatekeeper and brought Peter in. Then the maid who was the gatekeeper said to Peter, 'You are not one of this man's disciples, are you?' He said, 'I am not.' Now the slaves and the guards were standing around a charcoal fire that they had made, because it was cold, and were warming themselves. Peter was also standing there with them…

…now Simon Peter was standing there keeping warm. And they said to him, 'You are not one of his disciples, are you?' He denied it and said, 'I am not.' One of the slaves of the high priest, a relative of the one whose ear Peter had cut off, said, 'Didn't I see you in the garden with him?' Again Peter denied it. And immediately the cock crowed." Jn 18:15-18, 25-27

Jesus, **"Peter was one of My first disciples, and he was a very strong disciple. But he knew that he was strong, and this was his weakness. He did not have the humility of John or of My Mother, which is why he denied Me and could not stand by My Cross. In humility I am able to be strong in Love for you. Peter was to lead My Church, but for such a job he needed great humility. He needed to know the frail weakness of his body and heart, so that he could give it to Me and allow for My strength and Love to enter in. In that, I would guide My Church from within him. I allowed Peter to fall so that I could make him strong in My Love. My remedy to his sin would make him holier and stronger than if he had never fallen. I allowed him to** fall in weakness as an example to others; an example of My deep forgiveness which I offered him in My single look immediately after he denied Me. Oh that one glance of Love contained fathomless mercy for My disciple –and all of My people –whom I love and who deny Me in their weakness, wounding My Soul. If Peter would have received My mercy in full in that moment, he may have wept bitterly, but he would of remained at My side. Yet in his fear and pride he was ashamed and ran away, leaving his wounded Healer alone. Oh how I loved Peter. It pierced My Heart to see him wound his own. Yet I was to heal his wound powerfully in My Love. This is My first lesson in his denial. I ask you to please always receive the gift of My humility to your heart. Treasure this gift. When you know and give Me your weakness, looking to Me for strength, I can help you. My little Peter thought that he could defend Me, God. What he needed to do was ask My

Love to defend him from his own weakness. After his fall, this is what he would do.

This leads to the second mystery that I desire to open up to you from these passages today. Where did Peter look in My Passion? He looked at those around him, questioning him. And he looked at himself, in defense. He was not looking at Me in love, for Love, or for My help. The one time he did look to Me after he fell, he saw My Love and realized what he had done in rejecting it as help to his weak heart. He wept because he knew he needed Me, yet I was being led to death. His faith was not yet rich enough to understand that My death would give him the very help in Love that his weak heart needed. Oh, My Peter was always learning. Look to Me always, when you are being tried for Me. I, the condemned Savior, am your Master Shepherd, and I will always come to your aid to strengthen you in My Love.

When I had first predicted to Peter of his fall –a warning I gave him so that he could prepare in prayer for his battle ahead, it had been after My words about Love. I had told him that by Love people would recognize him as one of My disciples. And his great love of Me lead him to the high priest's house, causing him to be recognized. It was his love that gave him away. And this love growing in his heart, which was truly My Love within him, could have saved him from his fall if it had not been so weak. A person must give all of themselves to Love, or else his Love dies. This is what happened with My 'other beloved' disciple Peter –his love died and he denied. Yet he was so beloved to My soul, even in this his weakness, for he was so honest that he quickly recognized his fault after he had fallen. And he did what I did when I fell on My Cross' Path. He got back up and continued on. He looked to Me, to My Love, for his answer. And in My one look to him I was able to enkindle and enflame his love to tears –so greatly that he bitterly wept for Me Who so needed love and for his weak heart that was unable to give it. In the end Peter would grow and in allowing My Love to enter in and heal him, fill him, he would be a fire of My Love in the world, leading My early Church with My Light within him.

I ask you to love Me fiercely, with all you have and are, so that your love will not falter or die. More than that, I ask you to let Me do this work in you, taking all of you as a possession of My Love and filling all of you with her source of My Heart. My Love in you must be fierce, or you will die on the path of My Cross I wish to share with you. Simply fiat and receive all of Me to yourself in trust, however I wish to give My Love to you. With you as well, I am never sorry for your weaknesses. Your littleness and incapabilities in love do not disappoint or offend Me. What you do with these is what matters. I ask you to learn from your brother Peter, for you have a fiery spirit and strength as well. Never depend on it. You must always know your great weakness as a human and you must always bring your weakness into the light of My Church asking for My healing Love and strength to heal and carry you. Always look to Me and My Love and never at the world around you or to yourself in defense of their questions. You will never be on trial for yourself; you are not important enough alone to be. But you will often be on trial for Me; and in these moments let My Love answer for you. What if Peter would have looked to Me for strength in My Love before he denied Me. I could have and would have defended him, answering for him. For I am a good Shepherd and I always rescue My littlest lambs. And although Peter thought he was strong, he was so, so little in My arms. Learn from Peter and imitate his example of looking to Me, but do it always constantly in your life, and you need not fall yourself to learn. Know in humility how much you need Me, even in My persecuted weakness—especially in My ridiculed, suffering Love—I will be your strength.

I love you, My little spouse of Love, and I bless you in this last lesson from My Heart. Stay awake and watch, pray with Me in your Cross' night, and in this I will give you the sweet rest of My grace and Love to strengthen and carry you Home. Amen."

6) The Scourging at the Pillar

"Then Pilate took Jesus and had him scourged." Jn 19:1

"Therefore I shall have him flogged....." Lk 23, 16a

"....he had Jesus scourged..." Mk 15:15b; Mt 27:26b

"But he was pierced for our offenses, crushed for our sins, upon him was the chastisement that makes us whole, but his stripes we were healed." Is 53:5

Jesus, **"My scourging had a two-fold meaning. And I will explain this to you here. Yet you will not understand the depths of My body and soul's suffering in the scourging until you simply enter into these wounds yourself. You must simply allow Me to draw you into them. The words I give you now will help you enter these mysteries, yet My Love will guide you much deeper than My words, opening new shadows of My suffering Love to you each time. The first suffering of My scourging was My nakedness. They stripped Me to mock and beat Me. I stood open, naked before all men, to receive the abuses of their sins to My soul and body. My Heart and body stood open naked, as I allowed Myself to be emptied in order to love fully. They** bound Me. I, Who was Lord, the Maker of Heaven and Earth, allowed Myself to be bound by My creation. And I loved them, even in their sin. I ask you to live by My example of humility in this. As they tied Me to the pillar, their thoughts and words had already pierced My Heart open. I was scourged by their hearts' indifference and cruelty even before their weapons touched My body. As their instruments of torture were flung at Me, the pain shot through My entire body. Pieces of My flesh and splatters of My blood flew through the air. And My gentled spirit of Love was not able to pierce their hearts –there was nothing I could do to heal them, but to drink the entire cup that My Father placed before Me. This was My first Eucharistic sacrifice –and this was a great desecration of My gift of Love.

As I told you, My scourging at the pillar had a two-fold meaning. The first had to do with My separation from My Father. My body was stripped bare of its divine gift of beauty to be covered by the wounds of man's sin. And each whip that wounded My body brought with it an even deeper wound of dark blindness to My Father's Love to My soul. Each wound I endured for mankind was like great sin poured out on My innocence. And as I took man's sin upon Myself, I was separated from My Father's Love in a visible way. This sin and torturous darkness would only increasingly cloud My Heart's vision of Love as I embraced every wound deep to My Heart. Yet My Father's Love, completely invisible to Me from this moment, would sustain Me –We were still united as one in My obedient fiat. This suffering of blindness would help all those blinded from knowing My Truth and My Love; those who would travel the great night of faith. From mystics to the greatest sinners, My blindness from My Father's Love as I was covered by man's sin would go out as a Light to heal the world. This darkness all began in My scourging. And this healing Love of Mine would also touch those who whipped Me, as I loved them dearly, with all My Heart, as well. Like it says in the prophet Hosea, at the time these men who hurt Me and were healed from My wounds 'did not know that I was their healer.' (Hos 11:4c)

The second great meaning of My scourging had to do with innocence pierced. Mothers stood by with their children during all of My Passion, and I was crushed as I saw these children's innocence pierced by the sin around them. Here in My scourging, I too was scandalized by the sin of men's hearts; as I always had the pure Heart of a child. In these moments when My body was in crucifying pain, My Heart was turned to all of the children of the world whose innocence would be scandalized by sin. And I suffered greatly for them. The little bits of My flesh and blood that flew from Me in the scourging were My little Eucharistic offerings for My littlest ones in the world. Oh how I prayed that their hearts be spared the torturous temptations that I endured in My innocent suffering. I prayed that they would be able to forgive their persecutors and that they would find healing of their innocence in My blood, in My silent, gentle Love... Amen."

7) The Crowning with Thorns

"Who is this King of Glory? The Lord of hosts is the King of Glory." Ps 24:10

"Then the soldiers of the governor took Jesus inside the Praetorium and gathered the whole cohort around him. They stripped off his clothes and threw a scarlet military cloak about him. Weaving a crown out of thorns, they placed it on his head, and a reed in his right hand. And kneeling before him, they mocked him, saying, 'Hail, King of the Jews!'

They spat upon him and took the reed and kept striking him on the head. And when they had mocked him, they stripped him of the cloak, dressed him in his own clothes, and led him off to crucify him." Mt 27:27-31

"And the soldiers wove a crown out of thorns and placed it on his head, and clothed him in a purple cloak, and they came to him and said, 'Hail King of the Jews!' And they struck him repeatedly." Jn 19:2-3

"It was preparation day for Passover and it was about noon. And he said to the Jews, 'Behold your King!'"
Jn 19:14

"They proclaimed, 'Blessed is the King who comes in the name of the Lord.'" Lk 19:38a

"Pilate had an inscription written and put on the Cross. It read, 'Jesus the Nazorean, King of the Jews.'"

Jn 19:19

Jesus, **"As the soldiers began to mock Me, it was as if all of hell was unleashed on Me. The darkness moved in; the evil one furied around to torment, taunt and tear at My body and soul to see if I would break. Yet I did not respond. I sat there still, silent, almost willingly—in love—enduring all for the salvation of mankind. These were man's wickedest sins that were unleashed on Me in the crowning of thorns and mockery that I endured. A God spit upon by His creatures who He was trying to save. It was a hideous sight. The shadows of temptations swarmed around Me, as the darkness seemed to grip at My body and My senses as well. I felt lost in evil, and this sickened My soul more than the physical cruelty or words that the soldiers beat into**

Me. My Heart had to fight to fiat in great humble, obedient Love. All of My energy at this moment was on My Father, through faith in His Presence and guiding Love. I did not listen to their words, and I did not listen to all the noise the devil made trying to disturb My soul; I listened, in faith, to My Father's Heartbeat of Love. I listened in hope that His Love would conquer all darkness. I listened in Love, for all mankind, as My mercy flowed out in My blood.

My eyes streamed with blood from the crown which dug deep into My neck and skull. The physical pain of this made Me nauseous. My Heart cried tears of blood for those around Me, destroying their hearts as they mocked My Kingship which would judge their hearts one day. The pain, the Love, the humiliation, rejection and forgiveness dug as deep into My body and heart as those thorns on My head. And I was silent. I did not open My mouth, as I offered all in humble Love. Your love, too, must be so humble, little in its purity and open in docile vulnerability as Mine was in the Crowning. They will mock My Love in you as well. And you must allow Me to answer from within you, with the same patient mercy as I did in My Crowning...Go with My blessing."

8) Jesus is Condemned to Death

"With revilement and torture let us put him to the test that we may have proof of his gentleness and try his patience. Let us condemn him to a shameful death, for according to his own words, God will take care of him." Wis 2:19-20

"The stone which the builders rejected, has become the cornerstone." Mt 21:42a

"When Pilate saw that he was not succeeding at all, but that a riot was breaking out instead, he took water and washed his hands in the sight of the crowd, saying, 'I am innocent of this man's blood. Look to it yourselves.'...Then...after he had Jesus scourged, he handed him over to be crucified." Mt 27:24, 26b

"Pilate again said to them in reply, 'Then what do you want me to do with the man you call the King of the Jews?' They shouted again, 'Crucify him!' Pilate said to them, 'Why? What evil has he done?' They only shouted the louder, 'Crucify him!' So Pilate, wishing to satisfy the crowd, released Barabbas to them and, after he had Jesus scourged, handed him over to be crucified." Mk 15:12-15

"The verdict of Pilate was that their demand should be granted. So he released the man who had been imprisoned for rebellion and murder, for whom they asked, and he handed Jesus over to them to deal with as they wished." Lk 23:24-25

"Once more Pilate went out and said to them, 'Look, I am bringing him out to you, so that you may know that I find no guilt in him.' So Jesus came out wearing the crown of thorns and the purple cloak. And he said to them, 'Behold, the Man!' When the chief priests and the guards saw him they cried out, 'Crucify him, crucify him!' Pilate said to them, 'Take him yourselves and crucify him. I find no guilt in him.'... Consequently, Pilate tried to release him; but the Jews cried out, 'If you release him, you are not a friend of Caesar. Everyone who makes himself a king opposes Caesar.' When Pilate heard these words he brought Jesus out and seated him on the judge's bench in the place called Stone Pavement, in Hebrew Gabbatha. And he said to the Jews, 'Behold, your King!' They cried out, 'Take him away! Take him away! Crucify him!' Pilate said to them, 'Shall I crucify your

King?' The chief priests answered, 'We have no King but Caesar.' Then he handed him over to them to be crucified." Jn 19:4-6,12-13, 14b-16

"He was spurned and avoided by men, a man of suffering, accustomed to infirmity, one of those from whom men hide their faces, spurned, and we held him in no esteem...oppressed and condemned, he was taken away and who would have thought any more of his destiny? When he was cut off from the land of the living, and smitten for the sin of his people." Is 53:3,8

Jesus, **"Judgment is a very dangerous thing. By one's judgment he condemns and by his judgment he will be condemned. It is best to always leave all judgment to God – Who knows all things, Who is Truth and Who judges in mercy according to a man's heart. By their rash judgment, faulty from their hearts' sins, I was condemned to** death by the Jews. They had rather wanted for Me to die then for Me –something they could not understand and judge –to live, forcing them to repent in their dark ways. The sufferings I endured as I stood on the Stone Pavement hearing My condemnation to death were much deeper than the hundreds of voices and faces I saw before Me –people I had taught, healed and loved –screaming for My Death. Such rejected Love pained Me, yet the darkness of their hearts pained Me even more. I saw before Me all the innocent unjustly condemned to death, as a result of others' jealousy, pride and selfishness. I saw how dark and cruel humans' hearts could be –so closed and void of My Father's goodness and Love. I saw the regret so many of My children would feel, when after living such evil ways finally saw truth. I suffered for My Father – King of Glory and all creation –as His Kingdom was mocked and His Son –His Messenger of Love –beaten and killed, hung on a tree. Oh the darkness which began to invade Me in the Crowning only deepened, as the devil twisted men's thinking and tempted Me to believe My Mission of Love had failed and was hopeless. Hearing the voices of so many people I dearly loved –from all times and places—pleading for My death through their sin saddened your Savior's Heart unto death. What can My words explain about My suffering in My condemnation to death—the experience was deeper than words, something I therefore embraced in silence. From within My silent, submissive Love, My Father would conquer. In My silent suffering, all those without strength or courage to defend the innocent (as Pilate was weak) would find the source of all they needed. The moment of My condemnation was tragic—for God, judged and hated by men—was innocently condemned to a hideous death. Yet that moment was glorious, for in it My Heart was able to fiat deeply in obedient Love to embrace all of man's sins and sufferings to heal, save and restore the world to My Father.

I bless you as you enter deep into this mystery in your life, and I will carry you through it Myself as I open its mysteries to you through our union in experience. Amen."

9) Jesus Takes Up His Cross

"Yet it was our infirmities that he bore, our sufferings that he endured, while we thought of him as stricken, as one smitten by God and afflicted....We had all gone astray like sheep, each following his own way; But the Lord laid upon him the guilt of us all." Is 53:4,6

"So they took Jesus, and carrying the Cross himself he went out to what is called the Place of the Skull, in Hebrew, Golgotha." Jn 19:16b-17

"Whoever wishes to come after Me must deny himself, take up his cross, and follow me. For whoever wishes to save his life will lose it, but whoever loses his life for My sake will find it." Mt 16:24-25

Jesus, "And as I took the Cross upon My already open and bleeding back, I took the weight of man's sin upon My soul as well. Oh you cannot conceive the weight of such evil darkness. I carried My instrument of torture along with man's 'instrument of torture' –being sin. The price I paid in physical, emotional, mental and deep spiritual suffering in this moment was enormous and difficult –yet I would bear My Cross 1000 times again if it was needed to save just one soul. The guilt of the most hideous crimes committed in the history of mankind passed through the chambers of My open, tender Heart. How I strove to love in this moment; how I strove to forgive; how I strove to focus not on man's sin crushing Me, but instead upon the merciful forgiveness of My Father's Love, which I could not see or feel. And in My desire and attempt to love, to focus on only Love, I conquered all defeating satan's lies that I, too, had been condemned and abandoned by My Father and that all was in vain. I did not listen to the evil one cunning around Me; and I did not listen to those beating, mocking and spitting on Me as I made My way to Calvary. I listened in the silence of My Heart to hope, that the fiat of My obedient, forgiving Love in My Heart would conquer. I took up My Cross and the guilt of men's sin, freely. For Love is free, and My endurance of the Cross had to be free in pure Love to save mankind. I had prayed to My Father to deliver Me, and He heard My prayer, as He gave Me in My humanity the strength I needed to drink His entire cup of crucified Love. I was deeply hurt by those who stood on My path, wounding Me with the burden of so much sin. Yet My burden was made light by the grace of My Father's invisible Love, one with My Heart sustaining Me.

Never will your cross be too heavy for you if you remain nestled in My Heart, humbly trusting My Love to bear all for you. As you live with Me in My Passion, you too will be nailed to the cross you must carry by the sins of others; yet always look to My Love which will conquer in you, for it already conquered and healed all sin in My Passion and Death. As you share with Me in suffering, drink fully as well in My remedy of redeeming Love which will unite us deeply as one. And I bless you. Amen."

10) Jesus Falls Three Times

"A grave was assigned him among the wicked and burial place with evildoers though he had done no wrong nor spoken any falsehood. But the Lord was pleased to crush him in infirmity." Is 53:9,10a

"But you, Lord, My God…in your great mercy rescue me. For I am sorely in need, my heart is pierced within me. Like a lengthening shadow I near my end, all but swept away like the locust. My knees totter from fasting; my flesh has wasted away. I have become a mockery to them; when they see me they shake their heads." Ps 109:21a, 22-25

"I am the good shepherd. A good shepherd lays down his life for the sheep. And I will lay down my life for the sheep. This is why the Father loves me, because I lay down my life in order to take it up again. No one takes it from me, but I lay it down on my own. I have power to lay it down, and power to take it up again. This command I have received from My Father." Jn 10:11, 15b, 17-18

Jesus, **"Never be afraid to fall on your path with My Crucified Heart. You are weak and you will be even weaker as My sufferings and others' sins are placed upon** you. As you share in My sufferings as a victim of Love with Me, you share in the guilt of others' sins. But just as you did not commit the sin for which you suffer guilt with Me, so too you will not bear its burden or overcome it –you can't because you are such a weak, little human, a child. My redemptive Love will work in you, bearing all, conquering all, forgiving all. This work I call you to share in with Me is the work of My Love within you. And so never fear to fall in your weakness –it is beautiful to be so frail and without strength of your own. What I would like for you to reflect on is how you fall. Do you fall in pride or in humility? In your fall do you try to protect and defend yourself or do you fiat in trust, receiving all trials and weakness in your life as My will and trusting My arms to carry you in your fall? For I do carry you in your times of greatest weakness.

I fell for you, on the Way of My Cross, so that you would never have to fall alone.

No, you have the grace from My fall to never fall away from Me, simply with Me in your suffering. In this you have no sin. It is not a sin to be weak, especially if your weakness is full of great trust in My Love. I fell three times, yes over and over again in My bodily fatigue. And My soul fell into deep darkness as well, blinded by darkness, needing to make great strides of faith, hope and love to stand up and continue on. I have already shared much with you as to how falling to the ground physically increased My pain. And I will continue to reveal many of these mysteries to you as you rest in My wounds and allow Me to open them within you.

As My head fell hard to the ground My thorns ripped My flesh anew with wounds, sliding onto My face and into My mouth and eyes. The Cross, heavy on My shoulders and back, fell heavy on My spine causing Me to lose My breath. My knees and the entire front part of My body was cut open on the rocks in the dirt as My whole weight fell upon it. As I tried to stand I received kicks to My mouth knocking Me down anew. The blood from My wounds along with the dirt covering the ground made it impossible for Me to see well. My mouth spit forth blood as I coughed to find My breath. And I continued. I did not give up in weakness, yet continued on in great Love towards My place of crucifixion. I was spit on and mocked as many people yelled profane accusations against Me. I did not see My apostles on this path, for I had been abandoned by them, left alone. My Love was mocked, rejected and hated. And My Heart was full of such a dark loneliness and longing for My Father, Who also seemed to have left Me in this night. The guilt of man's sin weighed around My neck causing Me to fall three times, not only from physical weakness but also from grief over the state of so many souls whom I had to redeem by enduring their sin. Such suffering is so great to endure. The darkness and reign of evil in such sin pierced and wounded Me much more than the great physical pain I endured. Satan attempted to cover Me in temptations of doubt, despair and revenge. I only answered with My Father's great mercy and tender Love of forgiveness.

And My throat was deeply cracked and parched in thirst on this road as well. How I physically thirsted for drink besides that of My sores' mucus and blood. How My eyes thirsted to cry as My Heart wept for Love of My brothers. Yet they too were dried up. How My Heart thirsted to see Love, that Love that My Father created in the world, left in someone's eyes. How I thirsted for innocence as the guilt of man's sin pierced Me, laying heavy on My soul. How I thirsted to give My Love, to find a soul willing to drink of her delight and to respond to Me in Love. And as I fell, I saw all those who would fall in sin and I saw all those who would answer My thirst in Love and My Heart was torn between grief and joy, sorrow and hope. I fell, weak from man's cruel sin, but also weak from such powerful Love pouring through My soul.

I made all things new in My suffering and pain.

And as you join Me in My wounds, in My wounded Love, I ask you to hold on to that hope. I drank all of mankind's sins, weaknesses, temptations and sufferings to Myself so that I could make them new in My priceless wounds of Love. Enter that Love, a Love willing to endure and forgive all, just to save a few. A Love that desires to be one with her Beloved Lord and Spouse in the deepest wounds of His Heart as well as in the deepest forgiving, redeeming Love of His Heart. This all I wish to share with you and I will if you only open yourself up in deep trust of My Love and allow. I will make all new in My Love in you and through you as you embrace this heavy night of the Cross in My Love today. I bless you in our work of Love. Rest in Me and I will do all."

"Falling on the Way of the Cross"

Jesus, "The Cross crushed Me and I was too weak to stand. Suffering crushed Me, buried Me alive –and I, Who was God, the Creator of heaven and earth, was too weak to stand beneath the weight of My creation's sin and cruelty.

It is okay to be weak. In fact it is 'normal' to be weak when you are crucified. That is what I want to teach you through your meditation on this mystery now. When the entire world seems to weigh on your soul –remember that the pain you feel is really just My wounded Heart. Remember that I am simply sharing My Heart's wounds with you. When you feel My Cross crush you to the ground, please don't fear to fall. I fell. And I will come to save you. But I must teach you how to fall. It is like learning a martial art. There are 'techniques' that you can use when you fall that will prevent you from 'breaking your vocation' (just as such techniques help a man in martial arts to fall without being hurt or breaking bones). Using these tools which I will give you will not prevent you from suffering or feeling pain in your fall, because your vocation is precisely to feel and suffer My pain and wounds on the Cross with Me. If I took these, you would lose your vocation and union with Me. But these tools which I will teach to you will help you endure great boulders of pain without being totally crushed and destroyed. They will help you remain faithful, simply enduring in Love.

First, when you 'fall' under the Cross do not look at the ground beneath you nor at the cross crushing you. Close your eyes if you have to, if it is impossible for you to gaze upon the sky –heaven –above you. But whatever you do, do not look at the pain consuming you. If you do, you will lose the focus of My Love and then your suffering will be meaningless. You must remain united with Me at all costs—even if your senses 'look at the ground and the cross' (the pain consuming you) –you must keep your heart focused on Me through fiat. This little fight of fiat in your heart will be enough to carry you through the most hellish of storms. It will keep you close to Me and therefore I will carry you Myself.

Secondly, do not fear when you fall. Fear is like a prison or web that traps you and keeps you from Me. When you panic about your life in fear, you become paralyzed and unable to move forward in your vocation as I desire. When you 'fall' on your way of the Cross –do not fear –do not take it too seriously. Remember that I allowed you to fall for a purpose –in order to deepen your union with Me. Please remember the important lesson I showed you in church yesterday. Your weaknesses and sins are like dust that I can blow away off of you in one moment of time. They do not touch your heart or soul. Even your 'sins' –imperfections really –make you beautiful to Me, for they show Me how weak and frail you are –how much you need Me as your Husband and Savior. Your sins are simply mistakes—so do not panic about them. Do you know how much I love to come and clean your thoughts, emotions, body, spirit, heart and soul with the kisses of My Love? And this makes us one. When a husband and wife are together in marital love it seems like no other form of love could unite them in such closeness. But if the wife becomes ill and her husband must strip her, clean her –join with her in marital love while doing all for her –then their love is deepened and purified. And when I come to you in such love, I do not take a 'wash cloth' to clean you from your weaknesses and tears. I use My mouth. I kiss your entire body, heart and soul –My thoughts kiss yours and change you by filling you with Me. My emotions drip upon yours through kisses of love and your emptiness is filled. So please, when I 'open you' to My Love by allowing you to 'fall' on your way of the Cross –in your crucifixion with Me –do not fear or panic or cry about the fall. I allow this to make us more one. I allow this so that we will cling even more fully to each other –you cling to Me in need of My grace, care and love –and I cling to you as a good Shepherd caring for My most miserable, lost, scared sheep.

...And lastly, when you fall, please remember that your weakness and wounds are really disguises –masks –that cover unfathomable treasures. When you see that you 'fall' in your cross –the reality is that you are climbing so close to Me –for when you fall I swoop down and catch you before you hit the ground.

I love you and I bless you in this new lesson of love. Please lay down now and rest in Me –Who you don't see –but Who invisibly is close to you in reality. Amen."

11) Jesus Meets His Mother

"Then the angel said to her, 'Do not be afraid, Mary, for you have found favor with God. Behold, you will conceive in your womb and bear a son, and you shall name him Jesus. He will be great and will be called Son of the Most High, and the Lord God will give him the throne of David his father, and he will rule over the house of Jacob forever, and of his Kingdom there will be no end." Lk 1:30-33

"...and Simon blessed them and said to Mary his Mother, 'Behold, this child is destined for the fall and the rise of many in Israel, and to be a sign that will be contradicted (and you yourself a sword will pierce) so that the thoughts of many hearts may be revealed.'" Lk 2:34-35

"Standing by the Cross of Jesus were his Mother, and his Mother's sister, Mary the wife of Clopas, and Mary of Magdala. When Jesus saw his Mother and the disciple there whom he loved, he said to his Mother, 'Woman behold your son.' Then he said to his disciple, 'Behold your Mother.'" Jn 19:25-27

"Whoever loves me will keep my word, and my Father will love him, and we will come to him and make our dwelling with him...peace I leave with you; my peace I give to you. Not as the world gives do I give it to you. Do not let your hearts be troubled or afraid." Jn 15:23,27

Jesus, "My Mother is the beloved of My soul, for She always does what is pleasing to My Father. The night of My Cross did not only pain and grieve My Heart deeply as I was wounded by man's sin. It also greatly tortured the innocent tender heart of My Mother. She knew I had come to earth to suffer; we had spoken of it many times as I had also with My Apostles. Yet as hard as it was for us to speak of such things, it was even much more difficult for Her to endure them as She met with the Face of Her suffering Son on His way to die on Calvary. Yet She was My hope as She held in Her heart the truth of the hope I had given to Her as I spoke of My resurrection beforehand. Her heart felt helpless, as She knew as She met Me on My way that even one delicate stroke of Her love would give My wounds more pain. And so Her love, too, was held silent and still as our hearts kissed in obedient fiat Love to the Father through the meeting of our eyes. My

Mother not only endured My crucifixion with Me, but She also suffered My entire Passion with Me as She remained one with My soul through all. She suffered Her martyrdom with Me, as Her heart was crucified with Mine on the Cross. I left Her on earth to be Mother of the Crucified full of My Heart's Love. Oh how can I explain to you a meeting of such intimate Love that occurred between Her heart and Mine on My way to the Cross? Her love pierced and strengthened Me, as My wounded Love filled Her soul full. And somehow, beneath it all, Her heart found peace along with My Own in My blood.

... Today I ask you to drink the cup of My Mother, of Mine, and to live this station with Me, for Love of Me. You are to be My Face of Suffering Love, which unites with others as they meet you on your way to Calvary. Your heart will carry My glance of tender hope under your marred face and wounded soul. And My Mother will unite with you, in a deep glance of Love, saying 'fiat' with you, as you meet Her and Her within many other people on your suffering path. My Mother did not only offer Me the comfort of Love as our hearts kissed through our eyes –but I gave Her the great strength She needed to endure Calvary to the end. I could not see Her well, as My eyes were full of blood and dirt, but I allowed Her to look on Me in Love to receive strength. And My Heart saw Her so clearly, as it knew Her pure Love. I will always strengthen you in the same way. And when you are blind, know that the eyes of your heart can always look to Me in faith to receive strength. Be not Martha in prayer, but instead be Mary. Be My Mother Mary who rested at My feet, stumbling to My crucifixion, in attentive Love. In living all this, we are made one, united deeply as one. Amen.

Let My blessing sing My Fiat of Love within you. Amen."

12) Simon the Cyrene Helps Jesus Carry His Cross

"As they were going out, they met a Cyrenian named Simon; this man they pressed into service to carry his Cross." Mt 27:32

"They pressed into service a passerby, Simon, a Cyrenian, who was coming in from the country, the Father of Alexander and Rufus, to carry his Cross." Mk 15:21

"As they led him away they took hold of a certain Simon, a Cyrenian, who was coming in from the country; after laying the Cross on him, they made him carry it behind Jesus." Lk 23:26

Jesus, **"Simon was My face of compassion in the world. In Simon I showed the world what it means to love and help their Savior. Yes, Simon greatly helped**

My fatigued body in taking the Cross upon his own back for Me. Yet I greatly helped his soul in allowing him to partake, to physically share in the suffering of My Passion with Me. And he was the only person I allowed that grace at that time. Why did I share My Cross with Simon? Because He needed to love; He needed for his strength, as well as his humble soul's love, to be needed. This gesture of love he did for Me in helping Me carry My Cross allowed great graces to be shed on him, his sons and on My entire Church. For he taught through his example that it was not only possible, but very good to help his Savior suffering under the burden of his sin. Simon's compassion was shown in physical action, and this greatly pleased My Father. As I shared with him My Cross, I also shared with him My Love, the means he needed to carry it.

And what happened in My soul as he took the physical burden of the Cross from

Me? My Heart was heavied by the even greater darkness that encumbered Me. Satan tormented Me by saying that I could not complete the will of My Father because I was too weak. And temptations encircled My mind making Me dizzy falling to the ground. Yet My Heart continued on in faithful –even joyful –fiat to My Father as I was glad to take on Myself the temptations My brothers already had and would suffer. My body and soul were weak, but My Love was strong.

Do not ever fear to take other's crosses as a burden of your own if I place it on your heart. In this you show Me compassion, as Simon did. And in this I stretch your heart, making it even more capable of receiving My Divine Love, as I enter in to help you carry your Cross in Love. For your crosses in life are simply pieces of My Own. Be My Face of compassion in the world as I allow you to carry My Cross. Now rest your weary head, hand and heart in My Love.

And listen to Me teach you in silence. And I bless you. Amen."

13) Jesus Meets Veronica, Who Wipes His Face

"I gave My back to those who beat me, my cheeks to those who plucked my beard; my face I did not shield from buffets and spitting." Is 50:6

"Even as many were amazed at him—so marred was his look beyond that of man, and his appearance beyond that of mortals—so shall he startle many nations, because of him kings shall stand speechless;" Is 52:14,15a

"And whoever gives only a cup of cold water to one of these little ones to drink because he is a disciple—Amen, I say to you, he will surely not lose his reward." Mt 10:42

"…His eyes were like a fiery flame His feet were like polished brass refined in a furnace, and his voice was like the sound of rushing water…When I caught sight of him, I fell down at his feet as though dead. He touched me with his right hand and said, 'Do not be afraid. I am the first and the last, the one who lives. Once I was dead, but now I am alive forever and ever. I hold the keys to death and the netherworld." Rev 1:14b-15, 17-18

"His eyes were like a fiery flame, and on his head were many diadems. He had a name inscribed that no one knows except himself. He wore a cloak that had been dipped in blood, and his name was called the Word of God…He has a name written on his cloak and on his thigh, 'King of kings and Lord of lords." Rev 19:12-13,16

"I give praise to you, Father, Lord of heaven and earth, for although you have hidden these things from the wise and the learned you have revealed them to the childlike…Come to me, all you who labor and are burdened, and I will give you rest. Take my yoke upon you and learn from me, for I am meek and humble of heart; and you will find rest for yourselves. For my yoke is easy, and my burden light." Mt 12:25,28-30

Jesus, "I gave My face to Veronica to wipe as an act of love towards her. I let her love Me, as her heart was so moved to do. And her love was a great witness of hope in the dark night of the Cross. Her love was a little light, alongside Simon, My Mother and the weeping women pitying Me, a sign of My Love conquering in hearts even in the midst of such cruel hatred. I wanted to teach Veronica and the entire world a lesson on the cloth where I left the image of My face. I wanted to teach them that when they love Me and do kindness for Me, I leave the imprint on the 'cloth' of their hearts as a witness to their love. This is also to remind them in their times of doubt of My presence and Love with them. If My Father so graciously rewards a small act of kindness to one of his little ones because of My name, how much more was He to reward Veronica, and all those in the world, who courageously show Me compassion in My dark suffering. Veronica did not look at those screaming insults around Me; no, her only focus of attention was on Me and the miracle of Love I was living before her. If only more souls would love as she did; if only more souls would show Me the loving care, in My great suffering, as she did. I know you have always loved Veronica dearly. She always held a place close to your heart because of her courageous, compassionate love to your pitiful Savior. I call all people to imitate Veronica, yet in different ways. Some I call forth to love Me in My Passion by showing compassion to others –the poor and My little ones. Some I call to 'wipe My face' as they preach about compassion and My great act of Love on Calvary. Some I call to comfort Me by prayer for their brothers and sisters in the world who are so far from Me. Yet you, I call you to wipe My bleeding face and to comfort My weary Heart as My spouse, by simply surrendering to My Love and letting it capture and captivate you. You I call to imitate her love by imitating Mine—for I have called Veronica to wipe My face. It was My act of Love that worked through her heart; she simply listened and responded. I call you to share in My Passion with Me by simply saying fiat in surrender, in obedient love to My crucified body, heart and life opening within you. By resting with Me, your Spouse, in a union of Crucified Love you will give Me great comfort. You are to be a Victim of Love and Mercy with Me, on My way of the Cross. You are to suffer right along with Me, taking the sins of others into your heart to answer with great forgiving love. In this you will be My little Veronica, My 'true image' in the world. And in this you will please My Father. This is My work in you, as it was My work that called forth love from Veronica's heart on My Cross' journey. There is always conquering of Love, a great hidden beauty and a deep union with Me, your Savior, in the midst of My Passion and death in your life. Rejoice with Me, My daughter, My beloved spouse, that I have opened you so deep to share with Me My cup so full. And I bless you in My compassionate Love, so that in your living union with Me My compassion will be spread in the world. Amen."

14) Jesus Meets the Weeping Women

"A large crowd of people followed Jesus, including many women who mourned and lamented him. Jesus turned to them and said, 'Daughters of Jerusalem, do not weep for Me; weep instead for yourselves and for your children, for indeed, the days are coming when people will say, 'Blessed are the barren, the wombs that never bore and the breasts that never nursed.' At that time people will say to the mountains, 'Fall upon us!' and to the hills, 'Cover us!' for if these things are done when the wood is green what will happen when it is dry?" Lk 23:27-31

"If he gives his life as an offering for sin, he shall see his descendants in a long life, and the will of the Lord shall be accomplished through him. Because of his affliction he shall see the light in fullness of days; through his suffering, my servant shall justify many, and their guilt he shall bear...because he surrendered himself to death and was counted among the wicked; and he shall take away the sins of many and win pardon for their offenses." Is 53:10b-12

Jesus, **"My tender Love called to the women in the crowd following Me. They** heard My voice of Love, and because of this they cried. They saw the great contrast between the brutal treatment I received, the hatred surrounding Me, My marred face and the gentle response of completely merciful Love that pardoned all. Yet they cried for Me, as they loved Me; and what I tried to help them in through My words was to cry for the souls who committed the hideous sin which was visible, to a degree, on My body. I was not to be pitied, for I was a God-Man Who would conquer in Love. I wished to share My deeper sufferings with them, and so I showed them the ones to be pitied, themselves and their children –for it was their sin which crucified Me. Some of those present in My crucifixion and some of their children would tangle themselves so deep in their sin that as they saw the Light and Truth of My Love they would desire to hide from Me (asking the hills and mountains to cover them) rather than to bring their hearts wounded by sin to Me to heal, forgive, save and restore. They were to be pitied, all those whose love and forgiveness was less perfect than Mine. For as far as their love was from Me, that was as far as they would also be from allowing My Father to fill them full in the life to come. The sins of men, seen clearly in My crucifixion, would be so hideous that mothers would regret they bore children; they would see that a physical life is worth nothing if that person's spiritual life is not in union with God. I had great hope in My suffering of the Passion, as I held on in My will in faithful 'fiat' obedient Love to the truth that My Love was greater than sin, My Light brighter than darkness and My Truth greater than all the deceit and hatred around Me. Yet these women, how I pitied them, for they were so weak in their faith. They would lose hope in the darkness, they would despair in love. Yet when I rose from the dead I would restore all to them, as I restored Peter's strength, courage and love to be much greater than before he fell. In his and their wounds I would place My wounds to heal. But the darkness and regret they would suffer was worth being pitied for they did not endure it with My hope and Love. If these things happened when 'the wood was green', when I was among them visibly and the graces of My Father's Love so richly filling their hearts, how deep would the sin and darkness be when I was taken back to heaven, when I was not physically visible, when the wood of My Cross –once green with life from My blood, was 'dry'? Who would preach when My wood was dry? Who would spread My message of Love to the children of these women? Many would be needed. Would hearts be humble enough to answer My call of Love?

I ask you in your night of the Cross to never pity yourself –as I never pitied Myself. Look at those who wound you and pity their hearts –lost in sin, wounded in weakness or simply closed to the great mysteries of Love I share with you. Pity those whose sins pain you and make Me suffer in you. And rejoice in your suffering –for as you allow Me to share My Passion, opening it within you, you are allowing for Me to give life from My Cross –to allow My blood to flow on My Cross within you. This will water the parched, dry land of hearts in your world today. In this you will keep the dry wood of My Cross –so forgotten and uncared for by many –green with the life of My blood and Love flowing in you. Always allow My hope and Love to fill your heart in darkness. Always keep your wounds open, naked and vulnerable in the night, trusting that My hand holds and guides you in them. In this I can pour out My peace, hope, forgiveness, Love and truth through them making them not only bearable, but sweet drink to those in the world around you. I give you My blessing from My kiss on the Cross. Rest in Me always. For this and only this is to be your life's work. Amen."

15) Jesus Is Stripped of His Garments

"But I am a worm, hardly human, scorned by everyone, despised by the people. All who see me mock me; they curl their lips and jeer; they shake their heads at me. 'You relied on the Lord—let him deliver you; if he loves you, let him rescue you.'" Ps 22:7-9

"They stare at me and gloat; they divide my garments among them; for my clothing they cast lots." Ps 22:18b-19

"They divided his garments by casting lots. The people stood by and watched; the rulers, meanwhile, sneered at him…" Lk 23:34b-35a

"They took his clothes and divided them into four shares, a share for each soldier. They also took his tunic, but the tunic was seamless, woven in one piece from top down. So they said to one another, 'Let's not tear it, but cast lots for it to see whose it will be,' in order that the passage of scripture might be fulfilled." Jn 19:23b-24a

"Who, though he was in the form of God, did not regard equality with God something to be grasped. Rather, he emptied himself, taking the form of a slave, coming in human likeness; and found human in appearance, he humbled himself, becoming obedient to death, even death on a cross." Phil 2:6-8

"Behold, I stand at the door and knock. If anyone hears my voice and opens the door then I will enter his house and dine with him and he with me." Rev 3:20

"I was sleeping, but my heart kept vigil; I heard my lover knocking; 'Open to me, my sister, my beloved, my dove, my perfect one!

For my head is wet with dew, my locks with the moisture of the night. I have taken off my robe, am I then to put it on? I have bathed my feet, am I then to soil them?" SOS 5:2-5

"The man and his wife were both naked, yet they felt no shame." Gen 2:25

Jesus, **"I had you add these two last verses for a very important reason. I suffered greatly as I was stripped of My garments before My crucifixion in Love; I suffered from man's ridicule, impurity and hateful cruelty. Yet I did not suffer in shame. My body was a great gift from My Father, which allowed Me to make our Love visible, and I was not ashamed of this beautiful gift of pure Love. You must always look at this suffering of Mine in nakedness as a suffering of Marital Love. Up to this point I had suffered greatly, yet it was as if the preparation for My total gift of Self in Marital Love on the Cross. I had** to be naked in the night of the Cross, so that I could give Myself in total Love emptying out My life to My Bride –the Church –and all souls who wished to receive Me. My gift was for everyone. And it was Marital. You must see the deep beauty of My Love's Marital gift that night. I want you to see that passage from Song of Songs as all being spoken by Me. I come to a soul and present Myself in suffering Love. I knock at their hearts' doors by the voice of My wounds' tender Love. I stand prepared, naked, to enter and give Myself fully in Love –to dine with the soul at the table of My Cross' Marital Love. My hair is wet with the dew of My Passion, and as I am stripped of My garments I am prepared, in a way, in My bridal dress to give Myself fully to My beloved. I have spoken to you much about the mystery of My nakedness, My sufferings and great Love therein, yet I can speak more and more. For this mystery is feared and avoided by many, and yet so full of the pure Love which hearts need today. I was naked to bear My wounds naked and open to the world –to open their hearts to receive My Love and to love Me in return. I was opened bare –stripped of My clothes and stripped of My flesh –so that I could open up the most closed hearts. I was bare, docile and vulnerable in Love to call others to humble purity as well. I wanted to give all of Myself –to have no barriers between My body and heart and the many souls I would embrace in Love in My Cross' Night. As I press you to Myself in the night of the Cross, you too must be stripped naked so that nothing comes between our Love. To receive My Marital Love you must be naked in trust, open and vulnerable in My arms on the Cross. In this, My wounds will wound you, My Love unite and fill you, My Life pour into you and My Resurrection conquer in you. You must be willing to be that close to Me; and in this I grant you the deep, pure, selfless, merciful Love of My

Cross' night. That is all for now. Rest in My wounds, naked and one with Me. This is My blessing for you…Amen."

16) Jesus Is Nailed to the Cross

"Like water my life drains away, all my bones grow soft. My heart has become like wax, it melts away within me. As dry as a potsherd is my throat; my tongue sticks to my palate; you lay me in the dust of death. Many dogs surround me; a pack of evildoers closes in on me. So wasted are my hands and feet that I can count all my bones." Ps 22:15-18a

"…They crucified him…then they sat down and kept watch over him there. And they placed over his head the written charge against him: This is Jesus, the King of the Jews. Two revolutionaries were crucified with him, one on his right and the other on his left. Those passing by reviled him, shaking their heads and saying, 'You who would destroy the temple and rebuild it in three days, save yourself, if you are the Son of God, and come down from the Cross! Likewise the chief priests with the scribes and elders mocked him and said, 'He saved others, he cannot save himself...He trusted in God, let him deliver him now if he wants him.' The revolutionaries who were crucified with him also kept abusing him in the same way." Mt 27:35a, 36-42a, 43a, 44

"They gave him wine drugged with myrrh, but he did not take it. Then they crucified him." Mk 15:23-24a

"When they came to the place called the Skull, they crucified him and the criminals there, one on his right, and the other on his left." Lk 23:33

"And when I am lifted up from the earth, I will draw everyone to Myself." Jn 12:32

"There they crucified him and with him two others, one on either side with Jesus in the middle." Jn 19:18

"Thomas said, 'unless I see the mark of the nails in his hands and put my finger into the nailmarks and put my hand into his side, I will not believe'…and Jesus said to Thomas, 'Put your finger here and see my hands, and bring your hand and put it into my side, and do not be unbelieving, but believe.'" Jn 21:25,27

"And just as Moses lifted up the serpent in the desert, so must the Son of Man be lifted up, so that everyone who believes in him may have eternal life." Jn 3:14-15

Jesus, **"My hands and feet were pierced by nails; yet My Heart and soul were pierced by man's sin. After they had stripped Me, I was roughly laid on the ground. My hands and feet bound by cords** were tied to the wood of the Cross and then, one by one, they nailed My members there fully. As the metal went through My skin, it pierced deep into My nerves, cutting Me in shoots of pain throughout My entire body. The nail was first put into My right hand, which symbolizes all the suffering I endured for the sake of peace and unity not only between My children, but also within their souls, between them and God. I suffered to offer them peace in the hostility of their lives reigned by sin. Then My left arm was drug and stretched, dislocating it at the shoulder. This was a great pain that caused Me to feel the pain to My left hand to a lesser degree. My left hand was pierced for purity sake, to save and restore those attacked by evil temptations to sin and those especially lost in sins of impurity. Only a pure heart can see God, and so I suffered this pain to My left hand and shoulder to purify hearts, so dirtied by sin, so that My Love could enter in to heal, fill and restore them to the kingdom of My Father. Then one soldier roughly sat on My legs until My feet were arranged in the place of the nail hole. As My legs were stretched and moved this way and that, My whole body shook with pain, for the nails in My hands –which went directly through My nerves, were ripped and torn. As My feet received the blows of the hammer along with the nail piercing them in place, I suffered great torrents of pain shooting up into My back which I offered specifically for the gift of humility. Humility is a treasure offered by My Father to all souls, yet accepted by only a few. It is a virtue without which no one can come to Our Love. I, Who was the Son of God, folded My strong, mighty legs in humble obedience, giving up My Own control of My Life to trust only in My Father's plan of Love in My last and greatest moments of trial. My feet wounded open are a gift for My littlest ones for they are close to the ground where they can come to freely drink as they wish and need. If only My people would receive all the graces of humility that I offer from My feet wounds, it would be so easy for them to enter the Kingdom of My Father. Lastly, they stood My Cross upright. All the pain shooting from My nerves increased as My entire weight hung from them. It was a clamor of pain, a storm of pain, which racked My body, but more so My soul, in that moment. All seemed to be lost in crucifying pain, yet My little Heart beat on in praise and Love of My Father's will and glory. My soul prayed 'Alleluia', while My members began to die.

What is three hours on a Cross like? Every moment brings with it the newness of pains which will never heal, yet only open more and more until death. Time stands still in pain and seems almost irrelevant. I did not count seconds until the suffering would end; I Myself did not know when it would end. I waited in darkness for the Word and invitation of My Father. I did not count time, yet lived from breath to breath, from fiat to fiat, from Love to Love. I ceased living on earth in those moments, as My Love, obedience and forgiveness stretched from time into eternity restoring and healing all. Yet all I saw was blackness.

And ...yet...what does it mean to have the nails that fastened Me to the Cross pierce and stretch through the center of My nerves? It means that My pain and Love would reach every corner of My being, and restore all to My Life. As the nails pierced My nerves incredible pain shot through My entire body, connected by the nervous system. These were My most sensitive places which were racked with human suffering. As the nails pierced My body in My nerves, seeming to sweep away and consume Me in physical suffering, crucified Love, the most tender, open, sensitive, vulnerable parts of My mind, imagination and emotions were attacked by the torment of darkness, confusion and fear as well. My memory was pierced through her nerves, causing Me to 'forget' My Father's faithful Love, while My Heart still 'remembered' and believed. satan with his temptations and mocking ridicule entered into My Heart's deepest Loves –of My Father, My Mother, My disciples and friends –trying to separate and tear Me from the Truth of My Father's care of them. All in My life seemed to be wounded open in that moment, and this pain in the 'nerves' of My body and soul would stretch into time lasting many years as I remained pierced open in such deep Love in the Eucharist. Yes, My Resurrected Love would enter and heal. Yet this would be lived together with My Crucifixion. Yet I held onto the hope that as deep and far as My suffering stretched, I would be united with My Father in Faith of His Love carrying Me. This is your lesson for your life as well. It is very simple. As I share the deepest sufferings of My Cross' night's pain, they will resound in your body and soul in the center of your most vulnerable, sensitive nerves. They will seem to consume you. Yet you must remember that this is only My Crucified Love consuming you. In this I am moving deep into you in Marital Love in a dance of Love to fill you with all of My life –all of My Heart's Love. Remain open and receive Me, I ask this of you. As I move from simply kissing you on the external parts of your life deep into you, into the core of your being, I will place My Crucified Love, My Life, in the center of your nerves. This will shoot out consuming all of you in pain, in fiat. You will die in this way, in My Love, to My Love and for My Love and in this you will be made deeply one with Me in the night of My Cross. This will be your heart's joy as we will be deeply united as one. And as My Resurrection moves in to restore and conquer all, we will

be forever united as one in eternity. And I
bless you. Amen."

17) Jesus Offers Great Mercy From the Cross

"Love your enemies, do good to those
who hate you, bless those who curse you, pray
for those who mistreat you…be merciful, just
as your Father is merciful." Lk 6:27-28,36

"Then Jesus said, 'Father, forgive them,
they know not what they do.'" Lk 23:34

"Now one of the criminals hanging there
reviled Jesus, saying, 'Are you not the
Messiah? Save yourself and us.' The other,
however, rebuking him, said in reply, 'Have
you no fear of God, for you are subject to the
same condemnation? And indeed, we have
been condemned justly, for the sentence we
received corresponds to our crimes, but this
man has done nothing criminal.' Then he

said, 'Jesus, remember me when you come into your kingdom.' He replied to him, 'Amen, I say to you, today you will be with Me in Paradise.'" Lk 23:39-43

"Standing by the Cross of Jesus were his Mother, and his Mother's sister, Mary the wife of Clopas, and Mary of Magdala. When Jesus saw his Mother and the disciple there whom he loved, he said to his Mother, 'Woman behold your son.' Then he said to his disciple, 'Behold your Mother.' And from that hour the disciple took her into his home." Jn 19:25-27

Jesus, **"The merciful Love I lived in union with My Father stretched throughout all of My life and even deep into the night of the Cross. The more We were reviled and hated, the greater the portals of mercy that were opened from My Heart's wounds flowing out to restore those that sinned against Me back to life in** full union with Our Trinitarian Love. I did not come to earth simply to preach mercy, but to be mercy's living sacrifice of Love. I came to be mercy in the midst of a world which deep in its sin had forgotten mercy's name. And as they had forgotten to show mercy to others, they had completely lost their relationship to her, making it impossible for their hearts to receive Mine. A heart is opened to receiving mercy through showing it. As Dismas the good thief showed Me mercy on the Cross, his heart was opened to receive Mine. I prayed My prayer of forgiveness on the Cross for those who wronged Me, so that in asking mercy on their behalf –and in suffering for this request –their hearts would be opened to receiving the great gift of mercy My Father wished to share with them in My blood. And the gift of My Mother to John and all mankind was an action of My living mercy as well from the Cross. Mercy and forgiveness is not simply something someone must say or think, but it must be real, concrete, lived, visible. Forgiving Love must be visible. And so I gave My Mother to John and to all those in the world who had hurt, ridiculed or misunderstood Me. I gave Her as a gift of mercy that I knew would also be at times forgotten, ridiculed or misunderstood. But I gave My Love visibly in Her, for She lived mercy in union with My Heart always. She is the greatest gift of My merciful Love to sinners and all of mankind, for in Her they would find My compassion, forgiveness, humility and tender, pure Love after I was gone, after I had already died on the Cross. In Her, they would meet My promise and prayer of mercy, 'Father forgive them, for they know not what they do.' In Her they would find the refuge of My Heart's Love to care for their wounded souls and to encourage them, intercede for them, love them and heal them in My Name, through My blood which She ever treasured as She carried it in Her heart. I shed Her blood that day, as I received all My humanity from Her. And I shed your blood as well, as you and I have become one. I shed the blood of all martyrs –in blood and in Love –I shed the blood of all those who suffer and sin in the world, in order to make it an offertory to save them. And when you suffer as well in the dark night of your body and soul, you shed My blood in the world –for I have come to live in you profoundly –not only in My crucified, suffering Love, but also in My Eucharist. We are one in suffering, and we must be one in merciful Love. For the first is pointless without the second. And so I offer you tonight My great blessing of merciful Love –a Love that visibly lives forgiveness as an oblation for sin. And I ask you, as you enter and move deeper into My wounds, that you drink fully of the grace I give you to live My rich mercy in your suffering Love. In this your heart will be opened and stretched even wider to receive

My mercy –and in this we will be united as one. And I bless you, in My Name and Love. Amen."

18) Jesus Thirsts

"Like water my life drains away; all my bones grow soft. My heart has become like wax, it melts away within me. As dry as a potsherd is my throat; my tongue sticks to my palate; you lay me in the dust of death." Ps 22:15-16

"How long, Lord? Will you utterly forget me? How long will you hide your face from me? How long must I carry sorrow in my soul, grief in my heart day after day?" Ps 13:2-3

"After this, aware that everything was now finished, in order that the scripture might be fulfilled, Jesus said, 'I thirst.'" Jn 19:28

"Jesus, tired from his journey, sat down there at the well. It was about noon. A woman of Samaria came to draw water. Jesus said to her, 'Give me a drink.'" Jn 4:6-7

"Jesus answered and said to her, 'If you knew the gift of God and who is saying to you, 'Give me a drink,' you would have asked him and he would have given you living water.'" Jn 4:10

"To the thirsty I will give a gift from the spring of life-giving water." Rev 21:6b

"From noon onward, darkness came over the whole land until three in the afternoon. And about three o'clock Jesus cried out in a loud voice, 'Eli, Eli, lema Sabachthani?' which means, 'My God, My God, why have you forsaken me?'" Mt 27:45-46

"At noon darkness came over the whole land until three in the afternoon. And at three o'clock Jesus cried out in a loud voice, 'Eloi, Eloi, lema Sabachthani? Which is translated, 'My God, My God, why have you forsaken me?' Some of the bystanders who heard it said, 'Look he is calling Elijah.' One of them ran, soaked a sponge with wine, put it on a reed, and gave it to him to drink, saying, 'Wait, let us see if Elijah comes to take him down.'" Mk 15:33-36

"The one who sent me is with me. He has not left me alone, because I always do what is pleasing to him." Jn 8:29

Jesus, **"The darkness of My thirst was deeper than you could ever understand or know. For My thirst on the Cross reached as deep and far and wide as the unfathomable abyss of My Love. Yes, My thirst on the Cross was physical. My throat and entire body, emptied out of all its liquid through My blood, sweat and tears, was dried up as a desert without life. The** fire of My Love had embraced and consumed all. Yet the thirst I speak of in My words from the Cross is My thirst for Love. I thirsted for the drink of My Father's Love which would bring with it the Light of His Radiant Truth. I thirsted for mankind's love, so mixed up in selfish desires and motives; yet I thirsted for it to be pure. I thirsted for My Mother's Love and for all the just souls in the world. For it pained Me to see the great darkness and pain they would have to suffer on account of other's evil. I thirsted to give Love, to find souls waiting and ready to receive My Love's great depths and gifts. I thirsted for those too lost to thirst for Truth, for God, for righteousness. I thirsted for souls too wounded to even know to thirst for pure Love. I thirsted to make reparation for all the evil thirsts of deceit, lust and gluttony that tempted and ruled so many in the world. My thirst was of Love and in Love, and My Father answered My great call of thirst with the redemption of mankind.

Never fear to deeply thirst. Even if your thirst of and for My Love leads you to death as Mine did. For such a death is of and for Love –and therefore in Love. As you enter My Cross' great night of battle –a battle for Truth and Love, you will suffer great thirst in both your body and soul. Fill your thirst, which is My thirst growing within you, with the drink of My suffering Love. As you thirst you are emptied out and stripped open all the more to receive My healing Love deep within you to make us united as one body, one soul, one thirst. As I told you before, your thirst for Me will first purify you, and then it will turn into My thirst on the Cross –in this My thirst in you is My song of Love calling you forward into My arms, into our Marital Night of Love. Rejoice in My thirst for it is a deep sign of My presence and Love. I bless you with My thirst in My dark Love on the Cross. This thirst will lead you on a path deep into My Heart's innermost wounds, to the spring of My Love itself. Do not look away from this source, to the left or to the right of this dark, lonely path. Please simply look to My Love and remember that you cannot fall away from Me, for you are in Me, and one with Me, in your seemingly endless search and thirst in the night. Fiat in littleness, in trustful Love and rest in Me, your ever faithful Spouse of Love, as I take My rest in you. Amen."

19) Jesus Dies on the Cross

"Amen, Amen I say to you, unless a grain of wheat falls to the ground and dies, it remains just a grain of wheat; but if it dies, it produces much fruit." Jn 12:24

"Now the ruler of this world will be driven out. And when I am lifted up from the earth, I will draw everyone to Myself." Jn 12:36

"It was now about noon and darkness came over the whole land until three in the afternoon because of an eclipse of the sun. Then the veil of the temple was torn down in the middle. Jesus cried out in a loud voice, 'Father, into your hands I commend My spirit,' and when he had said this he breathed his last. The centurion who witnessed what had happened glorified God and said, 'This man was innocent beyond doubt.' When all the people who had gathered for this spectacle saw what had happened, they returned home beating their breasts; but all his acquaintances stood at a distance, including the women who had followed him from Galilee and saw these events." Lk 23:44-49

"But Jesus cried out again in a loud voice, and gave up his spirit. And behold, the veil of the sanctuary was torn in two from top to bottom. The earth quaked, rocks were split, tombs were opened, and the bodies of many saints who had fallen asleep were raised. And coming forth from their tombs after his resurrection, they entered the holy city and appeared to man. The centurion and the men with him who were keeping watch over Jesus feared greatly when they saw the earthquake and all that was happening, and they said, 'Truly, this was the Son of God!'" Mt 28:50-54

"He was in the world and the world came to be through him, but the world did not know him. He came to what was his own, but his own people did not accept him. And the word was made flesh and made his dwelling among us, and we saw his glory, the glory as of the Father's only Son, full of grace and truth." Jn 1:10,11,14

"When you lift up the Son of Man, then you will realize that I AM, and that I do nothing on my own, but I say only what the Father taught me." Jn 8:28

"Jesus gave out a loud cry and breathed his last." Mk 15:37

"When Jesus had taken the wine, he said, 'It is finished.' And bowing his head, he handed over the spirit." Jn 19:30

"This is My beloved Son, with whom I am well pleased." Mt 3:17b

"He will wipe every tear from their eyes, and there shall be no more death or mourning, wailing or pain, for the old order has passed away. The one who sat on the throne said, 'Behold, I make all things new.'" Rev 21:4-5a

Jesus, "My Spirit was always My Father's. He had given Me His Breath of Life in My Incarnation, and I never took My Spirit to Myself. I always allowed My Spirit to be His, as Our Holy Spirit of Love flowed freely between Our Hearts guiding My every step and word. It was His Spirit that held Me silent and it was His Spirit that gave life to My words, speaking from within Me. I had a work as I came from heaven, a simple work from My Father that I needed to accomplish with Him; this work was to proclaim His Kingdom and to redeem all of mankind back to His Love. When I finished all He had asked and desired of Me, I returned Home to Him. Your life is that simple as well –that simple of a story of His Love.

The darkness of My last moments stripped Me to My bones, bare of strength. My last cry as I gave up My soul to the one Who made and loved Me in My body's incarnation was the final cry of Marital

Love. I lived deep union with My Father always, as well as with My people to whom I became incarnated. I deepened that union in My Passion and Crucifixion, as our souls were pressed deeply together in the darkness of suffering Love's obedience. The deeper and closer I drew man's suffering and sin upon Myself, the fuller we were one. Yet in My final moments on the Cross, all of hell was in an uproar, as I was conquering, defeating sin and pain and death in the obedient surrender of Love. As all of hell was unleashed on Me, on My already weakened body, soul and spirit, My Heart beat wildly in Love for My Father, offering all of Who I was in deep union with Him, to keep union with Him. And as I poured My life out, I died in the ecstasy of crucified Love's pain. Just as a man gives his life of self-gifted love in the darkness of night, so too I was stripped and emptied out in My gift of life as I cried forth, one with My Father, in a suffering fiat Love. I ask you to imitate Me in this. As I gave My life to My Father, He gave Me the gift of His resurrected life to My soul. As I give My life to you, offering for humanity to partake in such intense Love with Me as a sacrifice of gift-love to the Father and to Me, as they receive My gift of life poured back into their dying souls, you receive My selfless dying Love to live, witness and give life from within you. I will take you to Myself in these very last moments of deepest suffering and pain, where the grinding teeth of hell were audible to My ears, because I don't want to be separated from you in anything. I want to share with you all of My Heart's Crucified Love. And in such darkness, as you feel the earth tremble and shake in your heart in the dark, know that it moves from My Action of Love pouring out My life within you. I lie with you, in you, in these moments. And in My work of surrender, I save and redeem the world. There is such great beauty in this dark night of 3:00. And I wish to open it all up to you.

Through My gift of saving Love I made all things new. My Love transformed all suffering, sin and death. My life on the Cross wipes every tear, giving fruit to last eternity. In the deepest of night's betraying horror, My Love conquered. And I ask you to live in this conquering Love. I draw you into it in each breath you fiat. I Love you, My dear little one, My spouse of love, My precious soul, precious as you desire and allow Me to open My Heart's secrets within you and you treasure them in My Light of pure beauty. Stay with Me in this night, now and always. All you must do is stay holding My hand, pressed into My side, and My Love will do the rest.

From My death on the Cross, I bless you in Love, Fiat. Amen."

20) The Blood and Water: Jesus' Heart Was Pierced Open in Love

"Now since it was preparation day, in order that the bodies might not remain on the Cross on the Sabbath, for the Sabbath day of that week was a solemn one, the Jews asked Pilate that their legs be broken and they be taken down. So the soldiers came and broke the legs of the first and then of the other one who was crucified with Jesus. But when they came to Jesus and saw that he was already dead, they did not break his legs, <u>but one soldier thrust his lance into his side, and immediately blood and water flowed out.</u> This happened so that the Scripture passage might be fulfilled: 'not a bone of it will be broken.' And again another passage says, '<u>They will look upon him whom they have pierced.</u>'" Jn 19:31-34,36,37

"Behold, he is coming amid the clouds, and every eye will see him, even those who pierced him." Rev 1,7

"<u>Come to me</u>, all you who labor and are burdened, and I will give you rest. Take my yoke upon you and learn from me, <u>for I am meek and humble of heart; and you will find rest for yourselves.</u> For my yoke is easy and my burden light." Mt 11:28-30

"Let anyone who thirsts come to me and drink." Jn 7:37b

"Then he took the bread, said the blessing, broke it, and gave it to them saying, *This is my body, which will be given for you;* do this in memory of me.' And likewise the cup after they had eaten, saying, '<u>This cup is the new covenant in my blood, which will be shed for you.</u>'" Lk 22:19-20

"In the beginning was the word, and the word was with God, and the word was God. He was in the beginning with God. All things came to be through him, and without him nothing came to be. What came to be through him <u>was life, and this life was the light of the human race; and the light shines in the darkness, and the darkness has not overcome it.</u>" Jn 1:1-5

Jesus, **"My Heart was pierced, wounded open many times, over and over again by man's sin in My Passion. And because it is important for humans to make their love visible, I did not want for this deepest Heart wound of Mine to be left hidden and unseen within Me. For this reason, My Spirit led the soldiers to pierce My side, allowing for My blood and water to flow forth –a living fountain of mercy for the whole world. I was to give all, pour out My entire life within Me and allow these wounds also to be naked and open to the** world as an invitation. In My wounded Heart was the witness of My humble meekness; in My wounded Heart was the testimony of My great merciful Love –a Love that truly gave life to all who came to drink from it. In My side, pierced by the soldier after My death, was made visible – one time only –the mystery of My broken Heart's Eucharistic Sacrifice. The Eucharist I celebrated on Passover Thursday I lived on this dark Friday. No, My gift of Love to the world did not end or pause with My death, as My disciples waited for My Resurrection. My gift of Love went beyond death, as mercy continued to be poured out in My blood and water; as mercy would continue to be poured out in My disciple's breaking of the bread.

The mystery of My Heart's wound –in the spiritual and interior suffering I endured as well as in the physical wound from the sword's blade—is a Eucharistic mystery. For My crucified Love is a

Eucharistic Love, and My Eucharistic Heart is crucified. This is a mystery which is ever so important not only for you, but for all people in My Church today. As I give Myself to them, as I lay on the altar before them, as I enter within them in Communion, the gift of My Eucharistic Heart is the gift of My wounded Heart, a Heart wounded for Love of them in order to heal, strengthen and encourage them on their life's path home. My Heart is a living invitation to all to enter into the mystery of Calvary with Me, to wash themselves in My blood, dress themselves in My Love and to be opened up to be fed and filled by My very life. I wish to place My living fountain of life-giving blood and water in each heart as they receive Me in the Eucharist. They may be wounded by My Heart's sores as they are pressed against My chest, but they will be healed by these as well. Wounds that heal –that is the gift I want to offer My Church, and that is the gift I am offering you today. I wish to be wounded one with you, into you, and you into Me, so that as we are healed our flesh, our love, our souls and hearts may truly be one. That is the mystery I give from Calvary's side. And that is the mystery I invite you to enter with Me today in your life. Are you willing to be deeply wounded in order to be healed one with Me? How great and deep, high and wide are you willing to let My Love fill and consume you –possess you and fire you one with Me? Go to My Eucharistic Banquet, and I will continue to teach you afterward.....

...My Eucharistic Heart is an invitation to you to always live with Me My Crucified Love. And each moment My crucified body, heart, mind and soul caress you, it is an invitation for you to live deeply united with My Eucharistic Heart's presence within you. I need you to live that fully one with Me at all times. The wound you see in My side, in My Heart, is the door to your

Home within Me and to our nuptial bed of Love. As the earth quaked when I died, pouring out all of My life to the Father, My Heart's 'ground' will shutter as you rest there, but this is only My Heart's beat of Love; it is the action of My Love with you, for you, pouring forth My life in you. As the veil of the sanctuary was torn in two, so too will you be stripped bare and torn open in My naked Heart, so we can be pressed together so close as one. And as it was dark on My Cross, so too My Heart's cavern will be dark, yet this is because you are hidden so deep in union with My Heart's Love that your union with Me blinds you of all senses. I do not want you to run from Me as I take you to Myself. You may not always recognize the form of My presence as I unfold My crucified Heart within you; and so I want you to live great docility and trust that I will not let you falter and accidentally go the wrong way. Accept all as My gift of Love and trust that I am guiding and ever carrying you. When difficult situations arise and people attack, accuse or misunderstand you, gaze in deep love at My Heart, hold on to My wounded flesh and drink fully this gift of My Heart's wounded Love; in My blood you will find peace. Do not fear anything or seek a defense. Your entire focus must be Love, resting and welcoming My wounded Heart in Love. In this will be your peace. I bless you tonight, in this one of your last lessons of My Cross—yet not one of the least. Each has a deep, important meaning for your life. And as you finish writing (reading) these words, I will one by one open these mysteries even deeper into your heart in the coming weeks. This is your preparation. Now embrace Me, all of Me, in great love; and fiat with Me, in the hope of My deep presence, union and Love with you in My Cross' night. Amen. Alleluia!"

21) Jesus Is Taken Down From the Cross and Laid in the Tomb

"When it was evening there came a rich man from Arimathea named Joseph, who was himself a disciple of Jesus. He went to Pilate and asked for the body of Jesus; then Pilate ordered it to be handed over. Taking the body, Joseph <u>wrapped it in clean linen and laid it in his new tomb</u> that he had hewn in the rock. Then he rolled a huge stone across the entrance to the tomb and departed. But Mary Magdalene and the other Mary remained sitting there, facing the tomb." Mt 28:57-61

"The next day, the one following the day of preparation, the chief priests and the Pharisees gathered before Pilate and said, 'Sir, we remember that this imposter while still alive said, 'After three days I will be raised up.' Give orders, then, that the grace be secured until the third day, lest his disciples come and steal him and say to the people, 'He has been raised from the dead.' This last imposture would be worse than the first. Pilate said to them, 'The guard is yours; go secure it as best you can.' So they went and secured the tomb by <u>fixing a seal to the stone and setting the guard</u>." Mt 27:62-66

"When it was already evening, since it was the day of Preparation, the day before the Sabbath, Joseph of Arimathea, a distinguished member of the council, who was himself awaiting the Kingdom of God, <u>came and courageously went to Pilate and asked for the body of Jesus.</u> Pilate was amazed that he was already dead. He summoned the centurion and asked him if Jesus had already died. And when he learned of it from the centurion, he gave the body to Joseph. <u>Having bought a linen cloth, he took him down, wrapped him in the linen cloth and laid him in a tomb that had been hewn out of the rock.</u> Then he rolled a stone against the entrance to the tomb. Mary Magdalene and Mary the Mother of Jesus watched where he was laid." Mk 15:42-47

"Now there was a virtuous and righteous man named Joseph who, though he was a member of the council, had not consented to their plan of action. He came from the Jewish town of Arimathea and was awaiting the Kingdom of God. He went to Pilate and asked for the body of Jesus. After he had taken the body down, he wrapped it in a linen cloth and laid him in a rock-hewn tomb in which no one had yet been buried. It was the day of preparation, and the Sabbath was about to begin. The women who had come from Galilee with him followed behind, and when they had seen the tomb and the way in which his body was laid in it, they returned and prepared spices and perfumed oils. Then they rested on the Sabbath according to the commandment." Lk 23:50-56

"After this, Joseph of Arimathea, <u>secretly</u> <u>a disciple of Jesus</u> for fear of the Jews, asked Pilate if he could remove the body of Jesus. And Pilate permitted it. So he came and took his body. Nicodemus, the one who had <u>first</u> <u>come to him at night</u>, also came <u>bringing a</u> <u>mixture of myrrh and aloes weighing about</u> <u>one hundred pounds. They took the body of</u> <u>Jesus and bound it with burial clothes along</u> <u>with the spices, according to the Jewish burial</u> <u>custom.</u> Now <u>in the place where he had been</u> <u>crucified there was a garden</u>, and in the garden a new tomb, in which no one had yet been buried. So they laid Jesus there because of the Jewish preparation day; for the tomb was nearby." Jn 19:38-42

Jesus, **"My dear little child, My dear little (one), there is a threefold beauty I wish to teach you about in this mystery of My body's burial. As the Gospel recounts, there was a garden in the place I was crucified—a symbol of beautiful life in the** midst of such ugly torture, pain and death. This garden was a symbol for My Love, which was the true hidden beauty in My night's Cross and pain. Always look for My garden of beauty and life, My fruitful Love, in the midst of the Cross. There you will find hope.

And so there are three little treasures of beauty in these passages about My burial. The first is found in Matthew's account that the Jews were afraid of My Resurrection, afraid I was right, afraid of My Love's conquering death; and so they requested that the tomb be guarded and it is recorded that a seal was placed on the rock of the tomb and a guard posted. This does not seem beautiful. It does not seem like something good, that I was sealed so tight, strongly hidden away even in My death, from people. Yet My Father used this for a glorious good –to show His power and glory. I was dependent, My body tightly locked away in the ground, on My

Father's 'defense'. And when He raised My Spirit from the dead, the Spirit I had given over to Him on the Cross, the seal and guard only testified even louder to My Resurrected Life. This is a deep lesson for you. When in your life people try to seal you up, hide you away tightly, even stand guard to watch your every move, do not fear or feel unfree –you are always free in My Love; and, because of these persecutions, My Father's defense of you will bring Him so much more glory. He will rescue you, He will deliver you in your night, He will conquer your death in Love, as He did for Me three days after I died. Let them tie you up and seal you in, guarding and judging, watching for your response. Look to My Father in a free spirit of peace and childlike joy, and He will deliver you in Love. Always. You are close to My body, still persecuted after death, and to My resurrected life and Love in this.

The second hidden beauty in My burial accounts has to do with Joseph of Arimathea, a 'secret disciple for fear of the Jews,' and Nicodemus who first came to Me at night. Both of these men, in My life, came to Me secretly hiding themselves in the darkness of night out of fear. Yet look what My Love did to transform their hearts in the Love of My night on the Cross. This second time they came to Me at night was not out of fear as the first; no, they came to Me in the night of My Cross in courageous Love and with great respect. They were not afraid in My Cross' night to be seen with My body; they were not afraid to witness to their Love, and to My Love. They were not even afraid of being accused of defying their law by caring for My body as the Sabbath evening approached. They gave Me all they had and they gave Me their best. They placed Me in new, white linens and in a new tomb. Their love was greater than the law, although they strove to respect that as well. Oh how My Heart rejoices as I think of the fire of Love in the souls of these two men who cared for Me in death.

And this leads Me to the third hidden beauty in this mystery of My burial. Each of the Gospels say something a little different –one says Joseph bought a new linen and laid Me in his new tomb; another refers to Nicodemus buying a hundred pounds of oils and myrrh and bringing them to prepare My body with Joseph. A third account says that the women, attentive to My need for a proper burial, went and collected spices to treat My body with. And all of these are true –and together they are beautiful. The work of My burial they did together, as a family. Yet it was more than just a burial, it was the first adoration of My body. Yes, as a Child the shepherds and wise men came to adore, yet they came to adore Me as a whole Person –body, blood, soul, divinity –all wrapped up in the Christ Child. This was beautiful and good. Even then their gifts of myrrh and frankincense foreshadowed My death, yet they were given to Me, not used to adore My body. There were other times in the Gospels where people did gestures of adoration towards Me; Mary crying at My feet washing them with her tears and drying them with her hair covering them in kisses; or when she anointed them with oil. But these too were not gestures in pure adoration of My body as being holy, as much as to Me as an entire Person. But here, in My death, My body is emptied of all life, My blood drained out, My Spirit given up to My Father. Yet, My body alone –even after death –called forth great praise, adoration and prayerful Love from the hearts of these people. Each brought Me gifts of prayerful Love from their hearts as they washed, dressed and cared for the body of their crucified Savior. Each gift was different –some brought linen, others spices, aloes, oils, myrrh –another the tomb itself; yet each was a beautiful expression of adoration love of their God-Man Savior's Body. My body alone was holy enough to be that honored. It is not an easy thing to take a person down from a Cross. Joseph suffered in great love in this. My body was completely filthy in dirt, sweat, blood and many open wounds; I smelled of death. Yet Joseph embraced this body of Mine in tender love, as he reached up unfastening first one nail, then the other, holding My body to himself in an embrace of Love while My feet were unfastened so that I would not fall to the ground. Then placing Me on the ground they washed Me; not with the normal necessary water, but as they could from the few jugs they had. Then they wrapped Me in a new, white linen cloth –as My body wounded open in Love in the Eucharist is often wrapped in the white altar cloths. I was dressed with aloes, perfumed oils and myrrh as My body is often adored with incense in adoration.

And I was then laid in the tomb, My first night in My tabernacle of Love, locked in with a stone. What great purity I pierced their hearts with as they were closer to My naked body then they had ever been before. Yes, those who dressed Me for burial received great graces of Love for their kind, generous hearts' work. What mercy they showed Me, their merciful Savior. What deep love I called forth from their hearts as they touched Me, caring for their wounded Healer. Yes, My Father's Love shed many graces on them in their work. And then they stood or sat in awe of all that had happened, and all they had done; some went home, others waited, not knowing what to expect, but truly pierced open to their hearts' core in Love. This mysterious Love I shared with them, even after My death, is a lesson of open, docile humility for you. And it shows to you the power of pure Love.

This is My lesson for you tonight. I bless you with My wounds, with My wounds that My friends adored, kissed and loved –bathed with their tears and dressed with perfumed oil from their hearts that Pascal Night. And I ask you to let Me set you that on fire as well, that you will never fear death, but instead know in your open, naked, pure love, I Myself will care for your body, dress your wounds and bring you in the tomb of My Heart where you will rise again with Me in Love. I love you. Take My kiss to your heart now and rest in Me. Amen."

XI

The Resurrection of Jesus

22) The Empty Tomb and Jesus Appears to Mary Magdalene

"After the Sabbath, as the first day of the week was dawning, Mary Magdalene and the other Mary came to see the tomb. And behold, there was a great earthquake; for an angel of the Lord descended from heaven, approached, rolled back the stone, and sat upon it. His appearance was like lightening and his clothing was white as snow. The guards were shaken with fear of him and became like dead men. Then the angel said to the women in reply, 'Do not be afraid! I know that you are seeking Jesus the Crucified. He is not here, for he has been raised just as he said. Come and see the place where he lay. Then go quickly and tell his disciples, 'He has been raised from the dead, and he is going before you to Galilee; there you will see him.' Behold, I have told you.' Then they went away quickly from the tomb, fearful yet overjoyed, and ran to announce this to his disciples. And behold, Jesus met them on their way and greeted them. They approached, embraced his feet, and did him homage. Then Jesus said to them, 'Do not be afraid. Go tell my brothers to go to Galilee, and there they will see me.'" Mt 28:1-10

"When the Sabbath was over, Mary Magdalene, Mary the Mother of James, and Salome bought spices so that they might go and anoint him. Very early when the sun had risen, on the first day of the week, they came to the tomb. They were saying to one another, 'Who will roll back the stone for us from the entrance to the tomb?' When they looked up, they saw that the stone had been rolled back;

it was very large. On entering the tomb they saw a young man sitting on the right side, clothed in a white robe, and they were utterly amazed. He said to them, 'Do not be amazed! You seek Jesus of Nazareth, the crucified. He has been raised; he is not here. Behold, the place where they laid him. But go and tell his disciples and Peter, 'He is going before you into Galilee; there you will see him, as he told you." Then they went out and fled from the tomb, seized with trembling and bewilderment. They said nothing to anyone for they were afraid." Mk 16:1-8

"When he had risen, early on the first day of the week, he appeared first to Mary Magdalene, out of whom he had driven seven demons. She went and told his companions who were mourning and weeping. When they heard that he was alive and had been seen by her, they did not believe." Mk 16:9-11

"While they were puzzling over this, behold two men in dazzling garments appeared to them. They were terrified and bowed their faces to the ground. They said to them, 'Why do you seek the living one among the dead? He is not here, but he has been raised. Remember what he said to you while he was still in Galilee, that the Son of Man must be handed over to sinners and be crucified, and rise on the third day.' And they remembered his words. Then they returned from the tomb and announced all these things to the eleven and to all the others...but their story seemed like nonsense and they did not believe them. But Peter got up and ran to the tomb, bent down, and saw the burial clothes alone; then he went home amazed at what had happened." Lk 24:4-9, 11-12

"On the first day of the week, Mary of Magdala came to the tomb early in the morning while it was still dark, and saw the stone removed from the tomb. So she ran and went to Simon Peter and to the other disciple whom Jesus loved, and told them, 'They have taken the Lord from the tomb and we don't know where they put him.' So Peter and the other disciple went out and came to the tomb. They both ran, but the other disciple ran faster than Peter and arrived at the tomb first; he bent down and saw the burial cloths there, but did not go in. When Simon Peter arrived after him, he went into the tomb and saw the burial cloths there, and the cloth that had covered his head, not with the burial cloths but rolled up in a separate place. Then the other disciple also went in, the one who had arrived at the tomb first, and he saw and believed. For they did not yet understand the Scripture that he had to rise from the dead. Then the disciples returned home." Jn 20:1-10

"But Mary stayed outside the tomb weeping. And as she wept, she bent over into the tomb and saw two angels in white sitting there, one at the head and one at the feet where the body of Jesus had been. And they said to her, 'Woman, why are you weeping?' She said to them, 'They have taken My Lord and I don't know where they laid him.' When she had said this, she turned around and saw Jesus there, but did not know it was Jesus. Jesus said to her, 'Woman, why are you weeping? Whom are you looking for?' She thought it was the gardener and said to him, 'Sir, if you carried away, tell me, where you laid him, and I will take him.' Jesus said to her, 'Mary!' She turned and said to him in Hebrew, 'Rabbouni,' which means Teacher. Jesus said to her, 'Stop holding on to me, for I have not yet ascended to the Father. But go to my brothers and tell them, 'I am going to My Father and to your Father, to my God and your God.' Mary of Magdala went out and announced to the disciples 'I have seen the Lord,' and what he told her." Jn 20:11-18

Jesus, "On the first day of the week I rose from the dead; not the second or third; not late in the day, but very early in the morning on the first day of the week. As soon as My people had been emptied and purified completely from My death, I came to give them My abundant life as well. I came to fill them. I want you to learn from these Gospel Resurrection accounts a great lesson of My Love, a Love that empties and purifies a person as it fills them. My death was not a happy experience for anyone; with it came many sorrows to many hearts whom I loved. Yet the pain and suffering they endured was important preparation of their hearts. I did not come to take all their suffering and pain away from them; that would be impossible in a world left free to love. Yet I came to them to be with them in their darkness and to transform it. I came to fill their darkness with the meaning of My dark Love. I had to make them empty of the world and of their own selfish desires before I could place My Love within them to live. And so on My Resurrection Day I allowed them—I led them—to find My empty tomb. My empty tomb is a symbol for your heart, as you journey from purification to union with Me in crucified Love. Your heart, too, will be empty. Just as My burial cloths were a sign I had once laid there, so too your heart has remains of My presence, a presence that entered your heart to empty it. It was dark when Mary and the women first came to anoint My body. It is dark in your life, too, as I have emptied you of yourself to anoint you with My Love. Yet when they searched for Me where I had earlier been lain –beneath the rock guarding the entrance, I was gone. I had not emptied the tomb to fill it with My resurrected presence. I had emptied the tomb –a place for the dead –so that My life could begin a new work of Love elsewhere. I left My tomb empty so that the women and My disciples would begin a search –

would leave the tomb which they saw with their own eyes was empty of My presence and Love –and would instead follow My instruction, follow their heart's thirst to meet with Me in the places I wished to give them new life –My resurrected life.

This may all sound complicated to you, but it is all very simple in your own life. I have emptied your heart, especially in the time you have spent with Me here in the desert –as you write of and offer Me your life from the past. I emptied your heart of your life, of your deaths, of your sufferings; and I leave your heart empty, now, so that you begin your search. My resurrected Love wants to be a new, crucified Love in your life. My union with you wants to take a new form. I leave your heart abandoned – free and empty of the world and yourself, but now also of My Love –to guide you to My Heart, the place of our meeting in new life. I have allowed you to suffer without Me, so that you would be purified and ready to suffer with Me. All is changing in this dark, early morning of seemingly empty Love; My life is forming new places of My Heart to meet with you within you. Many did not believe or understand My Resurrection at first; and you, too, will be saddened, confused or tempted to doubt in your first steps of our new Love. It will seem as if I left, yet really I have begun to unite with you. It will seem dark, as I place My blinding light within you. You, like Mary, will weep –not from sadness as much as from confused love. Yet I will say to you as well, do not cling to Me as you once knew Me. Do not try to hold Me back from giving you the fullness of My Love. This is not the end –our happy meeting beginning to take place now in the garden where I was crucified. I have yet to take you with Me to My Father. Let Me guide you farther, deeper. Do not weep over the little deaths in your past. Weep now for joy as I take you one with Me into My great suffering Love and death on the Cross –a place where death cannot ever reign again for I have already conquered it in full by My obedient Love. Do not stand in bewilderment, but run in obedience, going where I send you, as I sent My Apostles to Galilee to meet Me. I stand before you, My little (one); I am living within you even if you cannot always see Me. I am not living or entering your old, emptied heart, so do not search there. Listen to My words and obey in faithful trust. Go ahead to Galilee, go ahead in the rooms of My Heart in which I have prepared to meet with you. It was there I first gave you My Love, and it is there I am leading you Home again to be united in Love as one with Me in Eternity. I stand before you, holding you; listen to Me call your name and follow this voice, My voice, you know and love so well. In this your tangled love will be freed to move closer and deeper one with Me in our union of Love taking place now. Rest in these words a little bit, before you move to your next lesson with Me. Let Me open their meaning up to be fully living in you. And I bless you with My new Love, always new –leading you away from all you know to create a new life, a new meeting, a new heart of My Heart's Love within you. Go in peace. Fiat. Amen."

23) Jesus meets with His Disciples

"The eleven disciples went to Galilee, to the mountains to which Jesus had ordered them. When they saw him, they worshipped, but they doubted. Then Jesus approached and said to them, 'All power in heaven and on earth has been given to Me. Go, therefore, and make disciples of all nations, baptizing them in the name of the Father, and of the Son, and of the Holy Spirit, teaching them to observe all that I have commanded you. And behold, I am with you always, until the end of the age.'" Mt 28:1-20

"But later, as the eleven were at table, he appeared to them and rebuked them for their unbelief and hardness of heart because they had not believed those who saw him after he had been raised. He said to them, 'Go into the whole world and proclaim the gospel to every creature. Whoever believes and is baptized will be saved; whoever does not believe will be condemned. These signs will accompany those who believe in My name. They will drive out demons, they will speak new languages. They will pick up serpents with their hands and if they drink any deadly thing, it will not harm them. They will lay hands on the sick, and they will recover.'" Mk 16:14-18

"Christ died for our sins in accordance with the scriptures; that he was buried; that he was raised on the third day in accordance with the Scriptures; that he appeared to Kephas, then to the Twelve. After that he appeared to more than five hundred brothers at once, most of whom are still living, though some have fallen asleep. After that he appeared to James, then to all the apostles. Last of all, as to one born abnormally, he appeared to me." 1 Cor 15:3b-8

"While they were still speaking about this, he stood in their midst and said to them, 'Peace be with you.' But they were startled and terrified and thought that they were seeing a ghost. Then he said to them, 'Why are you troubled? And why do questions arise in your hearts? Look at my hands and feet, that it is I myself. Touch me and see, because a ghost does not have flesh and bones as you can see I have.' And as he said this he showed them his hands and his feet. While they were still incredulous for joy and were amazed, he said to them, 'Have you anything here to eat?' They gave him a piece of baked fish; he took it and ate it in front of them…then he opened their minds to understand the Scriptures." Lk 24:36-43, 45

"On the evening of that first day of the week, when the doors were locked where the disciples were, for fear of the Jews, Jesus came and stood in their midst and said to them, 'Peace by with you.' When he had said this, he showed them his hands and his side. The disciples rejoiced when they saw the Lord. Jesus said to them again, 'Peace be with you. As the Father has sent me, so I send you.'" Jn 20:19-20

"Thomas, one of the Twelve' was not with them when Jesus came. So the other disciples said to him, 'We have seen the Lord.' But he said to them, 'Unless I see the mark of the nails in his hands and put my finger into the nail marks and put my hand into this side, I will not believe; now a week later his disciples were again inside and Thomas was with them. Jesus came, although the doors were locked, and stood in their midst and said, 'Peace be with you.' Then he said to Tomas, 'Put your finger here and see my hands, and bring your hand and put it into my side, and do not be unbelieving, but believe.' Thomas answered and said to him, 'My Lord and My God!' Jesus said to him, 'Have you come to believe because you have seen Me? Blessed are those who have not seen and have believed.'" Jn 20:24-29

Jesus, **"In these Resurrection accounts I met with My disciples, My brothers and friends who had been with Me for three years as I prepared them for mission, My passion and death and resurrection. Yet they did not even understand or believe all that they saw with their eyes as My words were fulfilled before them. Oh the eyes are a funny thing, for at times they deceive us, yet at other times they build our faith. Yet if we believe because of what we see –the burial cloths, the empty tomb, My wounds,** then where is our faith? Sometimes eyes can hold a person back from growing in God, and that is what happened with My disciples. Yet I was ever so patient with their weaknesses. Where was My Mother all this time? Didn't She want to see My burial cloths, the rock moved from the tomb, My wounded body as proof for Her belief? No, Her faith was so strong that She always believed I would rise, for I had told Her that just as I had told My disciples. My resurrection was a truth to Her before She ever saw signs of it. Early that morning, even before Mary Magdalene had come to find My tomb empty, My Mother was rejoicing in wait for Me to come to Her. She believed My words and waited in joy for their fulfillment. Her love of Me erased all doubt.

I wish for you to believe in all My promises that I truly will come to you in deep union of Love, just as My Mother always believed. Before you see any proof of My presence, rejoice with Her, for the truth of My resurrected Love, of My union with you in crucified Love, has already begun.

I also wish to teach you about the power of My wounds. As Peter and John saw the linen cloth, stained from My wounds, they came to believe. It was the power of My blood and wounds that gave them such faith. As I appeared to My disciples and showed them My wounds, letting them touch them and place their hands within them, I completely transformed their unbelieving hearts. They were different men after their experience in My wound's resurrected Love. My wounds gave birth to faith. As you are wounded open, I desire for your wounds to be a source of great faith for the world. Do not hide them from other's hearts –let those with wounded faith touch them, pry them open, place their hands in them and nestle close with their own wounded souls. For these wounds of Love in your life are not your own, but Mine. Your body, heart, soul, entire life is Mine. And I have placed and will deepen My wounds within you, to unite you deeply one with Me in My Love, and to unite others to Me as well. You are like a tabernacle, or a monstrance, simply holding, living, displaying My living Heart and wounded Love to the world. Let them give birth to new life, in you and, in turn, in others.

Why did My resurrected body still have My precious wounds from the nails and the soldier's sword? It is because these were great witnesses of Love. These were the openings through which sinners could come to drink of My Resurrected Love. These are My battle-wounds of Love, witnessing to the depths of My and My Father's Love for each other and mankind. A lover never closes himself to hide from his beloved, yet instead remains open in a waiting invitation to pour out the gift of himself. Keep your wounds that I open in you always open to Me, waiting for My Love. Let Me heal you of your wounds by giving you My Own. Let Me touch and caress your hands, hair and face in My Love pouring from My open wounds. I will give you all of Myself to live in you. And as you receive Me deep to yourself in your answer and gift of Love, I will give and show Myself to the world through you. Now lay down in My wounds, always open in naked, vulnerable Love waiting for you to let Me give you the gift of possessing them. For you will possess them and all of Me through your deep Love. In this we will be one. Never tire of meditating on My wounds and of drinking from them as your source of life. For this is why I died for you—to give you free reign to all of My Love, all of Myself. Swim, live deep in My wounded-open Love for you. And I bless you, with My wounds, and in My strong faith of resurrected Love. Fiat, always. Amen."

24) Jesus Appears to the Two on the Road to Emmaus

"After this he appeared in another form to two of them walking along on their way to the country. They returned and told the others, but they did not believe them either." Mk 16:12-13

"Now that very day two of them were going to a village seven miles from Jerusalem called Emmaus...And it happened that while they were conversing and debating, Jesus Himself drew near and walked with them, but their eyes were prevented from recognizing him. He asked them, 'What are you discussing as you walk alone?' They stopped, looking downcast. One of them, named Cleopas, said to him in reply, 'Are you the only visitor to Jerusalem who does not know of the things that have taken place there in these days?' And he replied to them, 'What sort of things?'...

...And he said to them, 'Oh how foolish you are! How slow of heart to believe all that the prophets spoke! Was it not necessary that the Messiah should suffer these things and enter into his glory?' Then beginning with Moses and all the prophets, he interpreted to them what referred to him in all the Scriptures. As they approached the village to which they were going, he gave the impression that he was going on farther. But they urged him, 'Stay with us, for it is nearly evening and the day is almost over.' So he went to stay with them. And it happened that, while he was with them at table, he took bread, said the blessing, broke it and gave it to them. With that their eyes were opened and they recognized him, but he vanished from their sight. They said to each other, 'Were not our hearts burning within us while he spoke to us on the way and opened the Scripture to us?'" Lk 24:13,15-19a,25-32

Jesus, "I was opened up on the Cross, so as to open the closed hearts of men. I opened up My wounds to those I appeared to, to open their hearts in faith. And in this account of My meeting with these two men, My brothers, on the dusty road to Emmaus, I opened up My Eucharistic Heart to open their blinded eyes to My Light and Truth. Truly I celebrated the Eucharist on that road to Emmaus. Tired, weary and downcast from all that their lives had endured the previous few days, I came to them. I first opened their hearts through not only My presence which they did not know, but through My series of questions. I increased their thirst, their search for truth, love and wisdom as I walked along. I listened to their hearts' problems in patient trust that My Father would send Me His words in the Spirit to feed their hungry souls. After they had recounted all that had happened to them, I opened the Scriptures to their waiting hearts. As I fed them in My words, their hearts burnt to know more, to be closer to this One who came to save them. Their hearts burnt with the fire of My Love as we walked, and this Love opened them even more to receive the full gift of Myself. As I broke bread and gave it to them to eat, the Spirit of My Father's Love flew into their hearts reminding them of My broken Heart on the Cross. And in this they knew Me. In this they believed in the great plan of Love My Father had accomplished in the world through Me.

When you are tired and weary on your road come to My broken Heart for strength and light as well. I will guide you from within My wounds. When I come to you in a new form (as Mark's Gospel says), you will know Me by My broken Heart wounded for Love of you, and you must let My always new Love guide you. You must press so deep into My Chest, into My side, as we lay on the Cross as one, that your eyes can't deceive you or hold you back; for you follow and see with your heart, with and in My Heart and Love within you. When you meet with others on the road, tired and worn from their journey, listen to how My Spirit of Love wishes to open them first through your words, gestures, silence of prayer before you give them the gift of My Love within you. People must thirst to receive; they must desire to drink My Love in full. And most of all, as you travel on this road of Calvary's dark Love together with Me –within Me –please know that you will yourself be opened up, broken open in wounds that last, remaining open, in all pain and death and into My Resurrection. I will open Myself in you, to open other's hearts through you. As I remained open, naked and vulnerable in My wounds on the Cross to the thirst of those I knew needed My drink, so too will I hold you there one with Me. This is all, My Love. I bless you as you write these words of Love for Me. Your obedience is beautiful. Please take My blessing to your open heart to open you all the more full. Amen, Alleluia!"

25) Jesus Renews Peter's Love

"After this, Jesus revealed himself again to his disciples at the Sea of Tiberias. He revealed himself in this way...Simon Peter said to them, 'I am going fishing.' They said to him, we also will come with you.' So they went out and got into the boat, but that night they caught nothing. When it was already dawn, Jesus was standing on the shore; but the disciples did not realize that it was Jesus. Jesus said to them, 'Children, have you caught anything to eat?' They answered him, 'No.' So he said to them, 'Cast the new over the right side of the boat and you will find something.' So they cast it, and were not able to pull it in because of the number of fish. So the disciple whom Jesus loved said to Peter, 'It is the Lord.' When Simon Peter heard that it was the Lord, he tucked in his garment, for he was lightly clad, and jumped into the sea. The other disciples came in the boat, for they were not far from shore, only about a hundred yards, dragging the net with the fish. When they climbed out on shore, they saw a charcoal fire with fish on it and bread. Jesus said to them, 'Bring some of the fish you just caught.' So Simon Peter went over and dragged the net ashore full of one hundred fifty three large fish. Even though there were so many, the net was not torn. Jesus said to them, 'Come, have breakfast.' And none of the disciples dared to ask him, 'Who are you?' because they realized it was the Lord. Jesus came over and took the bread and gave it to them, and in like manner the fish. This was not the third time Jesus was revealed to his disciples after being raised from the dead." Jn 21:1,3-14

"When they had finished breakfast, Jesus said to Simon Peter, 'Simon, Son of John, do you love me more than these?' He said to him, 'Yes, Lord, you know that I love you.' He said to him, 'Feed my lambs.' He then said to him a second time, 'Simon, Son of John, do you love me?' He said, 'Yes, Lord, you know that I love you.' He said to him, 'Tend my sheep.' He said to him the third time, 'Simon, Son of John, do you love me?' Peter was distressed that he had said to him a third time, 'Do you love me?' and he said to him, 'Lord, you know everything; you know that I love you!' Jesus said to him, 'Feed my sheep.' Amen, Amen, I say to you, when you were younger, you used to dress yourself and go where you wanted; but when you grow old, you will stretch out your hands, and someone else will dress you and lead you where you do not want to go.' He said this signifying by what kind of death he would glorify God. And when he had said this, he said to him, 'Follow me.'" Jn 21:15-19

Jesus, **"It is very important for you to let people love you, to even call such love out** of their hearts. For Love heals and strengthens the human soul. I had already appeared to the disciples two times when I came to them again in this manner described by John. This time I did not come to My disciples to prove to them My Resurrection, for they already believed. I came so that My Love could in a special way move deeper into each of their hearts; and I came to heal Peter in My Love, for when he had denied Me before the bystanders during My Trials, he deeply wounded his own heart; and his heart remained troubled in its deepest core. I loved Peter most of all for his honest heart. He spoke the truth of how he felt and what he thought. He was very tender and open-hearted. Yet that is why he was so deeply wounded when he denied Me before others –in His words he denied Me from himself; he closed his heart refusing My Love which surrounded him trying to strengthen him. If he had just looked at My eyes, at My Love, before he answered the woman, he would have spoken truth. For he needed My Love to give him strength. Yet he was afraid and fell in weakness. Tell My people how much I dearly loved Peter through your embracing his answers to My questions of Love as your own. You, too, need healing in My Love from the times you wounded your heart in sin, in denial or disobedience. And so, with him, I ask you the questions I asked Him. I ask you to open your heart wider and wider with each answer, stretching yourself open in love to receive My Love. 'Do you love Me?' And in your heart's answer of 'yes', I ask you to feed My people with the Love I fill you with. You need My Love to be healed –because you need to love Me to be whole. When Peter saw Me and knew it was I on the shore, he did not wait for the boat to land but jumped in the water to swim to Me. His heart was burning to love and be close to the One Who he denied. As he was forgiven much –and he knew from our first meetings of My forgiveness for My Love spoke of it in My eyes –so he loved much. Yet his heart on the boat still needed something more from Me. And this is why he ran to Me. His heart had a thirst, a question, he himself did not know. And so I asked him if he loved Me. He needed to hear himself answer; he needed his love to be strengthened by his words. And then, I made a promise to him; a promise hard for him to swallow with his mind, yet which deeply rejoiced his heart's hunger to love Me. I promised him a death similar to Mine; I promised him that I would allow him to suffer and die for love of Me. And My conversation with him on the shore that morning, both in My words and the movement of My Heart's Love within him, healed and strengthened him to be the leader of My people. I did not simply ask him if he loved, but if he loved more than the rest. He sought the deepest, fullest Love; and this I granted to his heart.

And so, when people wound you and repent, you must call forth love from their hearts as well. You must let people love you, especially those weak or wounded in love and especially those who have hurt you. In allowing them to love you and in receiving their love as an answer to My Love in My Heart within you, My Love will flow back to them to heal and strengthen their Love of Me (and their love of Me in you.) In not only allowing, but calling forth love from them in simple, silent ways My Spirit will lead you in, you are making your wounds visible and vulnerable allowing them to touch even deep inside, so that their faith and love may be enkindled. You will teach people to love by letting Me work within you, as I worked with Peter. And My Love in you will meet with their wounded hearts making them strong and whole. You must let their love –which is My Love in them—pour forth fully. For in loving they will be healed and opened to receiving My Love deep inside as well.

And this is your lesson on Peter tonight. I bless you with My Love, the Love that tested him and the Love that conquered and strengthened in him. Fiat to My plan and will always. Amen."

XII

Litany of Trust

Heart of Jesus, most merciful,

-I trust in You.

Blood of Jesus,

-I trust in You.

Body of Jesus,

-I trust in You.

Wounds of Jesus,

-I trust in You.

Spirit of Jesus,

-I trust in You.

Hands of Jesus,

-I trust in You.

Feet of Jesus,

-I trust in You.

Memory of Jesus,

-I trust in You.

Word of Jesus,

-I trust in You.

Jesus, most humble,

> -I trust in You.

Jesus, most tender,

> -I trust in You.

Jesus, my Husband,

> -I trust in You.

Jesus, born in a stable,

> -I trust in You.

Jesus, little Martyr,

> -I trust in You.

Jesus, obedient Child,

> -I trust in You.

Jesus, in the Eucharist,

> -I trust in You.

Jesus, alone in the Garden,

> -I trust in You.

Jesus, scourged and abandoned,

> -I trust in You.

Jesus, mocked and crowned with thorns,

> -I trust in You.

Jesus, hated and misunderstood,

> -I trust in You.

Jesus, carrying the Cross,

Litany of Trust

-I trust in You.

Jesus, trusting the Father,

    -I trust in You.

Jesus, Love Crucified,

    -I trust in You.

Jesus, drinking Your Father's cup,

    -I trust in You.

Jesus, Resurrected,

    -I trust in You.

Jesus, send Your Spirit,

    -I trust in You.

Jesus, always with me,

    -I trust in You.

Jesus, always faithful,

    -I trust in You.

Jesus, always hopeful,

    -I trust in You.

Jesus, always forgiving,

    -I trust in You.

Jesus, always trusting,

    -I trust in You.

Jesus, my strength,

    -I trust in You.

Jesus, sing to me,
        -I trust in You.
Jesus, calm me,
        -I trust in You.
Jesus, be my silence,
        -I trust in You.
Jesus, be my peace,
        -I trust in You.
Jesus, be my light,
        -I trust in You.
Jesus, be my guide,
        -I trust in You.
Jesus, be my All,
        -I trust in You.
Jesus, be my Love,
        -I trust in You.
Jesus, my Beloved,
        -I trust in You.
Jesus, Jesus, Jesus,
        -I trust in You.
Jesus, Jesus, Jesus,
        -I trust in You.
Jesus, Jesus, Jesus,

-I trust in You.

Jesus, help me Fiat,

-I trust in You.

Jesus, take my fear,

-I trust in You.

Jesus, do all in me,

-I trust in You.

Jesus, rest in me,

-I trust in You.

Jesus, help me sleep in You,

-I trust in You.

Jesus, please give me the fiat, peace, love, joy, trust, strength, wisdom, humility and courage I need to suffer with you. Amen.

Additional Praise
for *Out of the Darkness*

"Mary Kloska has painted yet another wonderful icon as the title of this book. She provides a good explanation of the icon, which depicts Christ's love as gentle, humble and strong. Even though Jesus is shown on the cross and bleeding profusely, Mary shows us that He is in control. He looks at the scene in front of Him. It is as if He is directly looking in each person's eyes, who lived, is living, or will live. He looks into the eyes of the aborted and miscarried. He knows their need for salvation and sacrifices Himself. His strength is clear in that look, in the fact of giving Himself up, even more than the weakness of His of being crucified. That depth of profundity enters into the pages of the book and engages the reader, contemplatively. A reader cannot rush through the chapters. Every sentence must be thought about; every picture must be entered. Each section of each chapter builds on the next in a way that is deliberate and written with the attempt to bring spiritual understanding to the reader." – **Dr. Cynthia Toolin-Wilson, WCAT Radio host of "Author to Author"**

"This manuscript deeply affected me in my spiritual life… and it's very hard for an 82-year-old to learn anything new… this was really life-changing to my spirituality." – **Ronda Chervin, author of *Always a New Beginning: A Conversation Between Broken Catholic Spiritual Warriors***

"This book is a gift to anyone who reads it because it shows us how – as Jesus said to Mary – 'we can be profoundly made one' with Him on the Cross." – **Sr. Patrizia Pasquini, ASC, Generalate sisters of the Most Precious Blood**